Dr. Ray E. Short is highly regarded for his frank, honest answers to questions concerning sex, marriage, dating, love, and many other topics. He is also the author of *Sex, Dating, and Love: 77 Questions Most Often Asked.*

Here's what reviewers say about this book

Perhaps the best written and most thoughtful discussion of the issues involved in a dating relationship. The book offers the mature young person an excellent presentation of critical issues.

Christianity Today

The reader is treated with respect and candor. His discussion of sexuality is open and sensitive. What I see him doing is presenting a strong case for a sensible approach to sexuality and leaving room for the person to make the final decision.

Marriage and Family Living

This is a well-documented, straight-forward, explicit, unemotional treatment of the subject. It should be helpful for those who wonder if they are in fact, really in love. I recommend it highly for young people, and any uncertain adults.

Provident Book Finder

Dr. Short's book was one of the first to begin to turn around our culture from one that was sex-dominated to one in which now a more balanced view of sexuality is starting to prevail. Thanks to authors like Short, sexuality is beginning to be viewed in proper perspective.
The Catholic Herald Citizen

In an age when marriage is often undermined and sex outside of marriage is widely approved, it is refreshing to have some solid reasoning to the contrary.
Circle Magazine

A readable paperback tailored for young people—but of interest to almost everyone. A thought-provoking book—the distillation of material he has dispensed in marriage and family courses.
Milwaukee Journal

He uses facts and research to dispel myths held as truth by many young people. Short doesn't simply hand out answers, but he provides enough facts and logic for us to decide for ourselves.
Group Magazine

Parents, teachers, and counselors might well put the book into the hands of a young person contemplating marriage. It is written with taste and enough humor to provide a change of pace.
St. Paul Pioneer Press

Ray E. Short

Sex, Love, or Infatuation:
How can I really know?

AUGSBURG Publishing House • Minneapolis

To Jeannette and my mother,
and to Glenn, Linda, Ken, Tim, Karen, and Mary,
and to all who have ever wondered:
"Is this the real thing?"

SEX, LOVE, OR INFATUATION:
HOW CAN I REALLY KNOW?

Scripture quotations unless otherwise noted are from the Good News Bible, Today's English Version, copyright 1966, 1971, 1976 by American Bible Society. Used by permission.

Library of Congress Catalog Card No. 78-52180
International Standard Book No. 0-8066-1653-9

Manufactured in the U.S.A.   APH 10-5650

5 6 7 8 9

Contents

Preface

This innocent-looking little book has a past. Its roots reach back to my own fumbling, bumbling, often bitter attempts to sort out mixed-up romantic emotions in my youth. I later learned that this puzzled plight is shared by almost every other person who tackles the task of choosing a life mate.

And they do not seem to fare much better than I first did. Thousands are divorcing or living in unhappy homes. Many of those involved are sincere persons of intelligence, integrity, and goodwill—doctors, teachers, even ministers. The family itself is under fire. Why must so many face failure?

My resolve to write this book was born in a quaint village near Vienna. But my concern about the love problem harks back a quarter century to a student YMCA-YWCA summer conference in Colorado. P.K. Houdek of Kansas City fame gave us many inspired, sensible, useful hints on how to tell a real love from

7

a false one. His presentation not only helped solve some of my own problems, but it set me on a life-long search.

Houdek's unpublished analysis is still among the best, and by his kind permission, his study provides much of the framework on which this book is built. I am deeply in his debt—probably more than I know, since years tend to dim the sources of our ideas. So to P.K. Houdek and all those unknown others, I now render my warmest thanks.

If this book has a past, I trust it will also have a future. Not for the royalties it may bring—though authors enjoy getting paid just like anybody else. My hope is that it might give guidance to those who puzzle over the meaning of their own romantic emotions, as well as to those who counsel and care. My years of teaching dozens of college classes and of speaking to thousands of high school students have demonstrated a clear need. I hope this book will meet it.

Sex, Love, or Infatuation is meant not only for youth in search of solutions to personal plights. It is designed as well for use as outside reading in social studies and health classes, in courses of sociology, psychology, sexuality, and counseling. It can be useful as a special unit in mini-courses, church school and youth groups, summer camps and youth rallies or convocations.

Nor is it meant only for the young. It is for teachers and school counselors. It is for pastors and their spouses, for parents and families, and for advisors to all types of youth groups. Indeed, it is for all persons young or old who seek to sort out their own romantic feelings—or who care enough about the needs of others to want to help them do so.

Where case histories are cited, names have been changed "to protect the innocent"—though some of them are not all that innocent. And the book is written so it can be read by all ages from puberty on up.

Special thanks should go to Jeannette, my beloved wife, and to my family; to my colleagues at the University of Wisconsin-Platteville; and to the countless students in my classes and lectures through the years. All have been my teachers, and I am a grateful student. My thanks as well to Marnie Clark, Rod Bakke, Audrey and LoRee Haakonstad, Nancy Crowell, Lloyd Linden, Mary Russell, Jim Holt, the Stanley Moore family, Rhoda Voth, Cathy Pennekamp, the editors at Augsburg Publishing House, and all others who rendered help and encouragement.

But for any SHORTcomings or mistakes, I have only myself to thank.

R.E.S.

1 | Preview: The problem is personal

Once in a while some boastful young friend will brag, "You'll never catch *me* going bananas over some silly girl (or guy). I won't ever run around in a romantic fog. I'm never going to act like a love-sick puppy dog!"

We grin knowingly to ourselves. "That's what you think," we mutter under our breath. "Just you wait. Some day your time will come!"

And sure enough, it does. Sooner or later that person gets a bad bite from the love bug. He or she goes around in a hazy daze—ignoring friends, neglecting schoolwork, and bumping into tables in the library. Then none but the staunchest of true friends can resist the evil urge to say, "I told you so."

Just how likely is it that the "It will happen to you, too" forecast will come true? Modern research has come up with some surprising statistics.

Few will escape

Researchers have found that few people live out their lives without some romance, whether it be infatuation or real love. Several studies show that the typical American has from seven to ten romances over a lifetime. Sociologist William Kephart found that the average college student had already been infatuated six or seven times and in love once or twice. An average person will have about eight romances before marriage—and one and a half afterward! Further, almost half of Kephart's 1000 subjects said that at least once they had been infatuated or in love with two people at the same time.[1]

Eight romances, some of them coming in pairs! It seems that the lightning of love may strike not only twice in the same place, but many times over.

You have probably already had some of your expected allotment of romance. But if you are one of those to whom romance as yet remains a stranger, you need have no fear. The chances seem good that at some time, some place, it will happen to you. And probably several times.

The big question is, when the love lightning does strike you, how can you know for sure if it's the "real thing"? Is it the kind of love that can sustain a life partnership? Or is it just a passing fancy? There is no simple formula for figuring out the answer, but there are some very good clues. That's what this book is about.

But honey, you *will not* just know

Suppose you're a young girl and you think you might be in love. You finally develop the courage to ask your mother about it. "Mom," you say, "when

Dad came along, how did you know that he was really your Mr. Wonderful?"—assuming for the moment that he was.

Looking dreamy-eyed, Mom will likely give you her I-know-something-you-don't grin, and say, "Oh, never mind, honey. When it happens, you'll just know!"

Well, honey, you *won't* just know. Real love is more than a blinding flash of insight, a heart flutter, and a tummy twitch! The soaring divorce rates and high number of unhappy marriages show that people don't "just know" when it's real love.

What is this thing called love?

The word "love" has been used to describe all kinds of quite different things, from patient devotion to "lust at first sight." There's sexual love and there's mother love. There's brotherly love and there's married love. There's religious love and, perhaps most bothersome of all, there's romantic love. The list seems endless.

So how do we sort it all out? First let's take a good close look at the main offender, romantic love.

Romantic love: a lie and a hoax

Americans have long believed that romantic love is the sole sound basis for marriage. But is it really a firm foundation on which to build a life together? Let's look at just what this term means.

In "The Romantic Complex," Paul Popenoe lists some of the "planks" in what he calls the Romantic Love Platform:

> • Love is a mysterious visitation, which comes out of nowhere into the here and takes hold of you—just like the measles. [It] is recognized intui-

tively. . . . If it's the Real Thing, you won't have to be told. You will know without asking. . . .

• Love . . . is so important that you must give up everything else for it. . . . A man . . . is justified in giving up his wife. . . . A woman is justified in abandoning her home and children. . . . A king is justified in surrendering his throne for it. . . .

• It may go as unexpectedly as it came, and there is nothing you can do about that, either. It is not, in any way, subject to human control.

• You are not necessarily limited to one such episode. You can be a two-time loser, or a three-time loser, or a chainstore loser. . . . The intensity of [one's] own subjective sensations is the real measure of Love.

• [The person in love, like a tiny baby,] wants what he wants when he wants it, and is ready to sacrifice everything for the sake of his whims.

But Popenoe believes such behavior is wholly foreign to the idea of genuine love. He asks: "Now what relation has the Romantic Platform to St. Paul's words in the 13th chapter of [First] Corinthians? None whatever! The one is the antithesis, the negation of the other. And yet each purports to describe Love." [2]

For the reader who might have flunked Sunday school, here is a brief review of Paul's famous passage on love:

Love is patient and kind; it is not jealous or conceited or proud; love is not ill-mannered or selfish or irritable; love does not keep a record of wrongs; love is not happy with evil, but is happy with the truth. Love never gives up; and its faith, hope, and patience never fail.[3]

Some new definitions

It doesn't take an Einstein to see from Popenoe's planks that romantic love is not for sensible people.

It's much too weak to bear for long the full weight of a marriage. Isn't there something more solid? You can bet there is. It's called real love. First, some definitions.

Simple infatuation is often called a "crush" or "puppy love." It commonly strikes those in the early teens or younger. Usually the object of infatuation is some highly idealized person who is some years older —a teacher, an uncle or aunt, a friend of the family, an actor or actress. Simple infatuation seldom lasts long. But infatuated people may be greatly moved with emotion. They spend much time in daydreams and wishful fantasies.

It is not likely that these daydreams will ever be fulfilled. What chance is there that the student in junior or even senior high school will ever date, much less mate the teacher? Soon the fancy fades, and the person returns to reality.

Such tender feelings, no matter how strong, are not enough for marriage.

Romantic infatuation is what most people mean when they speak of "romantic love." Unfortunately, they often drop "romantic" and just call it "love," which is confusing. Romantic infatuation is the same as being "in love." It is what is meant when people speak of "falling in love." But alas, that is much like getting into a tippy canoe or hammock. If you're not careful, you'll fall right back out of it again.

Romantic infatuation is in fact a strange mix of sex and emotion—not genuine love at all. It will not of itself support a marriage.

Like the simple crush, romantic infatuation leads to idealizing the other person. It too is rooted in deep feelings. The difference is that in romantic infatuation these emotions may be much stronger and last longer.

15

At times they may reach fever pitch. The persons affected are normally a few years older and near the same age. They are likely to have a much stronger sex interest in each other than is the case in puppy love.

Romantic infatuation is therefore far more dangerous. The couple's desire for each other seems attainable, and they can more easily kid themselves into thinking they should go ahead and act out their intense feelings and sex urges. They find it easy to believe that they're old enough to know what they're doing. Sadly enough, they often aren't—and don't.

Such a couple may try to justify an early marriage long before their relationship has stood the crucial test of time. And even if they do avoid premature marriage, they may soon drift into a pattern of disapproved sex behavior before they are able to take full responsibility for their actions. Their bodies may have for the moment outgrown their minds and emotions. Hence, romantic infatuation can lead to a great deal of very deep trouble—and not just for the couple. It will affect their families, friends, and all who are close to them.

If you're struck by romantic infatuation, you will likely be just as unrealistic and idealistic as the one who has a crush. The added danger comes if you fail to see that your strong feelings are just not enough to support marriage or a long, intimate, total relationship. Infatuation is "pseudo-love" or false love. It is romantic quicksand. And woe be unto you if you mistake it for real love, then go on to act as if it actually were.

Romantic infatuation may develop into love, but it takes time, a lot of time. If you give a relationship a lot of time, you can be far more certain that your

16

decision about it is right. That makes the reward well worth waiting for, even if waiting seems painful.

Real love exists when your strong tender feelings for the other are balanced by reason and deep respect. You care just as much for the other person's welfare and fulfillment as you do for your own. Judgments about the person are quite objective and rational. The two of you have many values and ideas in common. You share similar goals and ideals. In short, you are matched as well as mated.

All these factors will probably be able to support and sustain a happy relationship over a long period of time. To the extent they can, it is real love.

The Greeks said, "Emotion must warm reason, but reason must rule emotion." That's a rule that can go a long way toward helping you handle your romantic experience wisely. If you're infatuated, your emotions will be in charge. In real love, your reason is on the throne, ruling your emotions.

One more type of involvement is often mistaken for love—*sex interest*. Sex is a deep biological drive that seeks some erotic expression. Usually there is a good deal of mutual sex attraction in every one of the three types of romance defined above. But the way the sex urge is expressed and the place it occupies in the relationship differs greatly with each type.

In addition, it is possible for people to enjoy sex with someone, yet have absolutely no other interest in them except sensual satisfaction. Because of our society's double standards, this is especially true for males. Most men can enjoy sex with a woman, yet have no tender feelings whatever for her. If this were not true, most prostitutes and massage parlors would promptly go out of business.

17

Sorting through the confusion

Both kinds of infatuation have one thing in common with real love: strong feelings of attachment to the other person. This makes it even more confusing to sort out the differences. Also, these three types of feelings are not mutually exclusive. They may overlap. The most passionate of romantic infatuations may include a measure of real love. And a deep love may contain some elements of infatuation. The differences between them may be more of degree than of kind. This makes it very hard to decide whether your feelings are primarily love or infatuation. All the evidence must therefore be examined with extreme care.

Almost nothing has been written solely to help typical persons sort out their different feelings relating to sex, love, and infatuation. While love is discussed at length, almost no studies have been done to understand the nature of infatuation. This is unfortunate, since infatuation is treacherous. It has caused no end of mischief and heartache to those who are caught up in its devilish deception. It is an attractive quicksand that lures its victims to marry, then sucks them down to despair.

"But wait," you may say. "Aren't you coming down a bit too hard on the idea of 'romantic love'? Isn't it the stuff that's supposed to make the world go around?" Certainly not. It may make heads spin on occasion, but not the planet earth.

The popular view that romantic love alone is enough for marriage is a vicious myth. This false notion must in fact take the lion's share of the blame for many if not most divorces and miserable marriages. It lures unsuspecting men and women into poor marriages like lambs to the slaughter. How long are we

18

to tolerate this threat to marriage? And what is more important, how can we avoid it?

I have an impertinent proposal: Down with romantic love! One thing we can do is to stop spreading the romantic love lie. If, as Popenoe claims, romantic love can end as fast as it begins, we should stop leading people to think it will last forever. If it is mostly selfish, let's stop telling people it is not. If it is not the same thing as real love, let's start making that quite clear. It is dishonest to continue such deceptions.

Another way we can clear up the confusion is to start saying what we mean. If the term "romantic love" is misleading, why not drop it? If the word "love" in that term leads people to think it means "real love" when in fact it only means "infatuation," it is a cruel hoax. It should be banned from the land.

So in this book the term "romantic love" is avoided wherever possible. In its place the term "romantic infatuation" is used. Let's label this myth "infatuation," which it is, instead of "love," which it is not.

I will put the term "romantic love" in quotes in the few cases where I do have to use it (when quoting another author, for example). By the time you finish the book, I hope you will have formed a firm habit of translating "romantic love" into "infatuation" whenever you come upon it. That will help you remember that they are two quite different things.

Researchers risk ridicule

Is the "love or infatuation" question such a big deal? A lot of people don't seem to think so. While you're sweating out a grim struggle with the question, you may be amazed to find that almost no one else even takes it—or you—seriously. Many otherwise very smart people will just dismiss your problem as either funny, silly, or hopeless.

Scientists have not felt free to make serious studies of love. A lot of people think that this subject is not worthy of such study. They scorn efforts to learn about romance.

Take this recent case. One of America's well-known senators is the Honorable William Proxmire. He made national headlines when he roundly chided the National Science Foundation for "squandering" federal funds. Why? Because it had made a grant aimed at serious study of "romantic love"—that is, romantic infatuation.

"I object to this," Proxmire says. "I'm against it because I don't want the answer. I believe that 200 million other Americans want to leave some things in life a mystery. And right at the top of things we don't want to know is why a man falls in love with a woman and vice versa. So National Science Foundation—get out of the love racket. Here if anywhere Alexander Pope was right when he observed, 'If ignorance is bliss, 'tis folly to be wise.' " [4]

Ignorance, Senator, is not bliss—it's risk. How can we ever hope to lower the rates of divorce and the misery in marriage by staying stupid? Research would well pay off if it helps keep people from making serious errors of mate choice. What price tag does one put on a broken home or a miserable marriage?

The Youth Research Center has found that almost half of the more than 7000 youth they studied "spent time every day (or quite often) wondering 'whether or not I will find a life partner.' " [5] It follows, then, that every time some new prospect for a romance comes along, you will raise the question once more.

"Could this really be it?" you wonder. And it's a very good question. If it is answered wrongly, it can lead to much sorrow or stark tragedy.

The old saying may be true: "If you marry on the strength of puppy love, you'll end up leading a dog's life."

In *His and Hers,* Dianne Kieren says those involved in a romance must face two basic questions: Am I in love? And if I am, what should I do about it? [6] This book is aimed at helping you answer those questions.

Why can't you just trust your heart?

Behind the "when it strikes you, you'll know it" idea is the assumption that your heart will somehow signal you when you've found real love. No one tells you *how* you'll know. They say, "You'll just know." Are they right? Can you depend on your heart?

Most youth think they're in love right now. If you're of late high school or college age, chances are better than even that you think you're in love this minute.

Albert Ellis asked 500 young women at 19 American colleges if they felt they were in love right at that time. A surprising 72% said they thought in some degree they were. Only 27% said they probably or certainly were not. [7]

But while most youth may think they're in love, they are at the same time not sure. About a third of the young women could only guess about their romantic condition. They said only that they probably were or were not in love. If we add this group to the 23% who thought they were "pretty much" in love, well over half were not at all sure. And we may reasonably assume that at least some of those who reported being in love were in fact only infatuated.

Most youth aren't sure what love is

William Kephart asked college students, "Do you feel that you know what love really is?" [8] The results were:

	Males	Females
I'm sure I know what love is	25%	36%
I think I know what love is	59	54
I don't think I know what love is	12	8
I'm sure I don't know what love is	4	2
	100%	100%

Note that more than two out of three are not sure they know what love is. They only think they do or do not know. Other studies have also shown that people don't know the nature of love, even when they're engaged. A study of hundreds of engaged couples who later married showed that a large proportion of the men, and even more of the women, had real doubts about their choice of a mate.[9]

Few love affairs—even the torrid types—lead to the altar. Gilbert V. Hamilton found that the subjects he studied had 6.7 romances each. Only 15% of the affairs led to marriage. And a study of the courtship patterns of 400 college students found that almost three fourths of their 582 love affairs broke up before marriage.[10]

Leonard Benson recently did a casual study of 75 students over 30 years of age. He found that they had had a total of 653 romances. That's an average of 8.7 affairs per person. Benson notes that in over a third of his sample the most intense romances did not lead to marriage.[11] Cupid is stupid, it seems—or at least unreliable.

Youth are not sure how to distinguish a pseudo-love from the real thing. Kephart's study found that students tend to think of their current romantic involvements as love, but they rate their past affairs as just infatuations.[12] Don't you suppose that many of these past "infatuations" would have been described as "love" if the persons had been asked to rate them while they were in progress?

So what does all this prove? It seems to show that American youth—and probably their parents and grandparents—are very unsure of themselves concerning love. They don't really know what love is.

It seems clear that "romantic love" (romantic infatuation, that is) cannot be trusted. If you can't trust your heart, what can you trust? What are you to do when you find yourself caught up in a romance? Most of us need help to decide whether what we feel is actually love. We need a reasonably accurate, rational way to determine the difference between love and infatuation during the period of the romantic involvement itself.

Age and maturity give no immunity

But isn't romantic infatuation only for the very young? Or for those who haven't grown up emotionally? It seems not. Even the most mature are not safe from the siren call of romance. Haven't all of us seen middle-aged or older couples with stars in their eyes, acting every bit as foolish as any teenager?

Or the rich old duffer who squanders his fortune on some sweet young thing? Such affairs happen just often enough that folk wisdom has long since declared: "There's no fool like an old fool!"

In our society the wedding ceremony is supposed to dry up all the springs of romance. But does it? In

23

the Benson study people reported having an average of one romance *after* they were wed. While most marrieds reported no other romances at all, some had as many as five. Luckily, few of these were acted on and they did not disrupt their marriages, but they did occur.[13]

Even the matured get lured

If you're more grown-up in your emotional life than most other people, you're still not protected from romance. When D.G. Dean set out to test the common assumption that "romantic love is for the emotionally immature," he found that it just isn't so.[14] The real test of emotional maturity then is apparently not whether you "fall in love" (become infatuated). That happens to almost all of us. The true test of maturity is rather what you do about it. Do you react rationally to this romantic condition? Or do you rush rashly into some foolish, perhaps permanent commitment before the relationship proves to be sound?

So expect romance—and be prepared

Romantic experience catches up with all of us, young or old, rich or poor, mature or immature. And with it come perplexity and uncertainty. If romance hasn't reached you yet, just be patient. Your time is coming! And if it has already come to you, it will likely come again—and yet again. The issue, then, is how can you act wisely once you are, as Capellanus put it, "wounded by one of love's arrows"? [15] You need something better than a soft-eyed grin and the old "never mind, honey; when it hits you you'll know it" routine. When you ask us an honest question, you deserve an honest answer.

2 | The crisis: Problems of partnership

You must make at least three big decisions in your life:

- Whom or what shall I serve?
- What shall I do with my life?
- With whom, if anyone, shall I share my life?

These are urgent questions for youth. All three choices will likely have to be made at a rather early age. Most people will have made them, in fact, before age 21 or 22. That's a big responsibility, since the consequences may follow you for the rest of your life.

Whom or what shall I serve?

Whether you realize it or not, you will probably adopt some central purpose for your life. You will build your whole life around whatever has the most meaning and the greatest importance for you. This will be your life center, your major focus.

How can you find out what your central value is?

Simple. Ask yourself: "What's the last thing in this world I'd be willing to give up?" Is it friends? Family? The chance to help other people? Devotion to God?

One thing seems certain. The kind of life you will have will depend on the kind of life center you choose. A life devoted to seeking personal pleasure will be far different from one committed to the service of others.

So your choice of a central life value—whom or what you serve—is crucial. It is not a decision to be made lightly or just drifted into.

What shall I do with my life?

What will your occupation be? That choice is of vital importance, since you will spend so much time at it. In fact, if you sleep the usual 8 hours out of each 24 and work at least 40 hours per week, that means you will spend half of your waking hours every work-day doing that job, and far more time if you choose a job like farming or homemaking.

So just think! If your job does not excite or challenge you, you've sentenced yourself to long years of being bored and unhappy with it. You'll scarcely be able to stick it out until quitting time, then you'll dash for the door. Is that any way to have to spend half the time you're awake on every workday of your life?

But if you're smart and choose your occupation wisely and well, then that same big block of time will fulfill and even excite you. The late Hornell Hart used to tell his students, "If you choose wisely your vocation, you'll never need a vacation." Perhaps he overstated the case. Yet few will deny that the wise choice of work can make a great difference in the amount of challenge, satisfaction, and joy you will have in life.

With whom, if anyone, shall I share my life?

Some people prefer not to marry, and that is certainly an acceptable choice. People should not be pressured into marrying if they prefer to stay single. For them, the third great decision will be *whether* to wed.

A few young people are experimenting with alternative life-styles such as the commune or living together WBC (Without Benefit of Clergy). But studies indicate that 9½ out of every 10 Americans marry.[1] Hence, the third really great decision for most people is the choice of a mate. Who is the best person to team up with for the rest of your life?

Just think. That will be the person with whom you plan to spend most of your adult years in the most intimate of all relationships. It is the person with whom you may co-create your children and share your life at every level. Choosing a mate is a decision to challenge your very best judgment. And a wrong choice can spell tragedy not only for you and your spouse, but also for your families and friends. It will be even more tragic if you have children.

Even outsiders have perceived our problem. "America appears to be the only country in the world where love is a national problem," observes Raoul de Roussy de Sales. "The great majority of Americans of both sexes seem to be in a state of chronic bewilderment" regarding love.[2]

An American folk song sadly laments, "Twenty years with the wrong woman." Well, *one* year with the wrong woman—or the wrong man—is far too long! One of the surest ways to avoid that tragedy is to be careful in choosing your life mate in the first place.

One thing seems clear, then. These three choices are important life decisions. If we choose poorly on any one of them, we cut down our chances to claim our share of self-fulfillment, meaning, and happiness throughout our lives. And who needs that?

What help can you expect?

Help with vocational choice abounds. Young Americans are urged to give a great deal of attention to the choice of life work. You can also get aid in choosing a life center. There's help from thousands of churches and synagogues, and colleges have departments in philosophy and religion. Yet if you look for help or training in how to choose a life mate, you'll be hard put to find it. What does the typical high school or college offer to help you choose a mate? Little more than a single course or part of a course.

And if there is a course, it may well be taught in home economics. If so, the men are likely to avoid it in droves. Ross Stagner notes that we send children to school for 10 or 15 years to learn a vocation, yet we teach them absolutely nothing about marriage, which is far more important than any profession.[3] He calls this "remarkable stupidity."

A plea for preparation

All this has led this student of family life to propose that no person should try to claim the high privilege of marriage unless he or she has had either a good course in marriage and family preparation or something equal to it. Divorce rates are lower for those who have had such courses. They do seem to help.

And if you can't take such a course? You can still get plenty of good guidance. There are now many fine books in this field. Some are listed in the back of this book. Most librarians, counselors, or ministers can place one or more such books in your hands. All you need to do is ask.

What is a successful marriage?

A marriage must have two qualities if it is to be pronounced a success by the general American public. It must be happy, and it must be permanent.

In our culture, husband and wife are expected to get along, to adapt to each other's needs. It is assumed that enough real love is present to bring joy and fulfillment to both of them. In short, the marriage should be happy. If it isn't happy, it's not a success. And if the marriage ends in divorce or if the two separate, we conclude that it has failed.

The soiling of the dream

Almost all of us want to marry. Most of us will do so at least once. But if current trends hold, that gentle wound from Cupid's arrow will become for many a painful thorn in the flesh. What begins as beautiful may become boring. Her Mr. Grand may turn out to be Mr. Bland, and his Miss Lovely has a good chance of becoming Mrs. Lousy.

The result can be predicted. Many who in their wedding vows agreed to swear *by* their commitment soon find that they are swearing *at* it. They become disillusioned, dissatisfied—and divorced. Their marriages move from rapture to rupture.

Your marriage may or may not be made in heaven, as tradition suggests. But one thing is certain. You will have to live it out right here on earth. What starts as marriage bliss tends to get constantly clouded by the routines of day-to-day living. Problems come up with disgusting frequency.

This is to be expected. After all, very few people in this world have no faults. Your chances of linking up with an angel seem slim. You can expect problems of adjustment. There will even be some friction. But just how often do such problems change a couple's cozy dream nest into a nightmarish den of conflict? If and when you wed, what are your chances of failure? The higher those odds are, the more careful you will need to be in your choice of your mate.

Divorce: our runaway rates

The prospects for marriage success are not rosy. One out of each three Americans who marry will be divorced in less than a dozen years. Some will marry and divorce several times, a practice which is sometimes called "legal polygamy." If we put all this together, the divorce rate is found to be about 41%. And it's still on the increase.

As of 1975, census reports show that the trend toward ever higher rates of divorce is worldwide. But the United States has the highest rate of all. Further, the divorce rate is going up faster in the United States than in any other country.[4] We are number one—an honor many of us would no doubt be glad to forego.

Many hang in there—and hate it

High as they are, the divorce rates do not tell the whole story of marriage failure in America. Many couples—about 3%—simply separate. Their rift is never entered in the official records. Divorce may be rejected by them for reasons such as convenience, money, religion, or simply neglect. Such marriage failures never get to the courts.

There is another, much larger block of marriage

failures: couples who stay together, but don't like it. About 15 to 20% of our marriages are unhappy unions which go unbroken.[5] They stay together because of the children, their religion, money, poor divorce laws, or some other reason. They just grit their teeth and stick it out.

Your chances are 50-50

Now let's put these various pieces of the puzzle together. Just what are the odds that you will have a happy marriage?

Take the 32 to 41% of U.S. marriages that are now ending in divorce. Add to that the 3% who separate and the 15 to 20% who doggedly stick it out, but are not happy with their choice.

The forecast is now clear. If you are typical, when you choose a mate *you will have no more than a flip of the coin chance that your union will be happy and for keeps.*

The teen marriage mire

If you marry as a teenager those odds are much worse. Then you take *twice* the risk that it will end in divorce and failure than if you marry in your 20s or older. Girls who marry before age 18 take even greater risks. They are three times more likely to be divorced than females who marry at ages 22 to 24.[6] One study found that many who marry as teens and do stay married tend to wish they had waited to wed. Almost half of the couples who married in their teens said they would not have married if they had it to do over again.[7]

How can we account for the fact that early marriage is so hazardous in America? There are a number of related factors.

31

Why early marriages often fail

1. A lot of early marriages are brought on by pregnancy. Such "forced marriages" have a very high risk of failure.[8] Yet 47% of the pregnancies in high school marriages take place before the wedding.[9]

2. The person who is immature in age is likely to be immature in emotions as well. As a result, he or she is more likely to make an unsound mate choice.[10]

3. Parents often object to early marriages—except in some cases where the young woman is pregnant. Then they may give their reluctant consent. Marriages that are entered when the parents are opposed, for whatever reasons, fail far more often than marriages where parents approve.

Parents have been known to go to great lengths to break up the marriages of underage youth. They even resort to legal means at times. If parents would try to help the underage couple instead of trying to interfere, these marriages might turn out better. In some cases the immaturity of the couple seems to be matched by the immaturity of their parents.

4. Early marriage tends to interfere with the plans for continuing the education of the breadwinner. This may in time saddle the marriage with serious money problems and lead to resentment.

5. One partner may work while the other continues with schooling. In such cases their interests often tend to grow apart. This in turn places added strain on the marriage.[11]

6. Early marriages tend to occur more often among the poor, so many of those who wed young have to face severe money problems.

7. Some teenagers hurry into marriage as an escape.

They may be fleeing a parental home they feel is too restrictive. This happens more often with females than males, since many families place more harsh restraints on girls than on boys.

8. Some women may engage in what has been called "the flight into intimacy." That is, they retreat into marriage because they are afraid to go it alone in a complex, tough world.

I know one girl who was a victim of "smother love." She had been severely dominated by her mother. One night she confided to her fiance: "Oh, John! I'll be so glad when we get married. Then I won't ever have to make any more decisions!" Needless to say, John ran away from her like a scared jackrabbit.

9. Finally, teen marriage failure may become a kind of self-fulfilling prophecy. That is, the couple and those close to them know teen marriages fail much more often. Knowing that, they may put forth less effort to keep such a marriage from failing.

On the other hand, knowledge of the dangers of early marriage may have just the reverse effect. The couple may see the handicap as a challenge. They may set out to prove to themselves and others that their decision to marry young was a smart one. They may get stubborn and refuse to give up. They want to show the world that, in the words of a song made popular by Nat King Cole, "We were not too young at all." [12] More power to them!

A call to caution

So persons who marry in their teens are just asking for trouble. They assume a terribly high risk of failure. In spite of that, almost half of U.S. marriages involve a teenage girl.

Don't be in a rush to marry. There's a mountain of evidence showing it's unwise. To marry too early is like spitting in a tiger's face. You may get by with it. A few do. But don't count on it. The odds are against you.

Ask yourself the question, "Would I choose the same kind of marriage partner at age 25 as I would as a teenager?" Chances are you would not. Studies show that as American youths get older their views toward love grow more realistic.[13]

We could not in every case advise: "When in doubt, don't." That dictum would be too rigid and harsh. There may be special factors in a given case—though you should not just assume that you're an exception to the rule.

What we do suggest is this: "When in doubt, delay!" Take your time—*lots* of time. Tread water for a while. See what the passing of time does to your relationship. Does delay tear it apart? Or does time let it blossom and become more beautiful?

Delay can be frustrating now. You may feel that you just can't wait to get married. But it may be well worth your while to hold off on your decision. After all, if your choice is sound, you have a lifetime to reap the rewards. But if your choice goes sour, the harvest holds little but regrets.

When rapture turns to rupture

Marriages, like nuclear bombs, produce a great deal of fallout when they explode. There is often a long period of bitter bickering before the break. Marital problems affect the couple's social life and their work. Both mates and their children experience a great deal of emotional (and in some cases physical) pain. This

34

spills over and affects most of the people close to them.

You may hear a lot about rational, sensible divorces. Why can't people go merrily on their separate ways with no regrets and no scars? It sounds right and reasonable. In practice it almost never happens.

Divorce starts a nearly endless circle

Marriage failures seem to beget more and more failures. Divorces—like good marriages—tend to run in families. If you have grown up in a family where both parents were very happy with their marriage, your views toward marriage will tend to be positive. That is one of the very best assets you can bring to your own marriage.[14]

Other factors of your past home life will also affect your own chances of marital success. You are far more likely to have a good marriage if (in order of importance):

- Your parents are happy in their marriage.
- You had a happy childhood.
- There was a lack of conflict with your mother.
- Your home discipline was firm but not harsh.
- You had a strong attachment to your mother.
- You had a strong attachment to your father.
- There was a lack of conflict with your father.
- Your parents were frank with you about sex.
- Your childhood punishment was infrequent and mild.
- You have an expectant, positive attitude toward sex that is free from disgust or distaste.[15]

Can the "inevitable" be changed?

Does all this mean that you cannot build a good marriage if most or all of these family background factors are against you? Certainly not. Even if all of them are negative, you may well be able to turn the odds around. But you will have to work harder to make sure yours is a good marriage. And you will have to be even more careful than most people to make sure that your mate choice is a good one.

The great American marry-go-round

The pattern of having many marriages and divorces during one's life is often identified with certain Hollywood and TV stars. I call these unions "revolving-door marriages." They constitute the great American marry-go-round. Persons who practice this pattern have several spouses—one at a time. A spouse is looked on in somewhat the same category as an automobile. You use it until the novelty wears thin. Then you trade it in for a fresh model.

It is of some interest to compare this Hollywood type of revolving-door marriage to the current trend of just living together. In reality, this trend is another type of marry-go-round, a revolving-door marriage without legal papers. Couples who live together take a "let's try it out first" attitude. But the motives of the two sexes for living-in are quite different.

Mattress hoppers

At Ohio State University a study was made of couples who were living together. The study spanned three different time periods. One goal was to detect trends.

Live-in males with previous
live-in experience

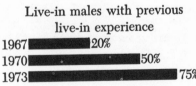

1967 ■■■■■■■■20%
1970 ■■■■■■■■■■■■■50%
1973 ■■■■■■■■■■■■■■■■■75%

In only six years the number of live-in males who had formerly lived with at least one other female rose from 20 to 75%! That's a huge jump of 267%! Scientists rarely find such a rapid change in any type of social behavior.[16]

It appears that the men are more and more engaging in what I call "mattress hopping." They're moving from one bed partner to another—with little or no intention of wedding any one of them.

Living together—for what?

The differing intentions of men and women in living-in arrangements were shown clearly in a Boulder study. There the most frequent reason the women gave for living together was that they were looking toward marriage. But the men? You guessed it. Their most frequent motive was simply sexual convenience and pleasure. One male put it very bluntly: "If you're living with a chick, it's a lot easier to get laid!" Well, that takes care of her hopes of marrying him! [17]

Small wonder that one of the most common complaints of live-in women is, "I sometimes get the feeling I'm being used." [18] Dearie, there just may be a reason for that. Many men seem to feel: "Why marry her if I can get all the advantages of marriage without taking any of the responsibility?" Why, indeed. Your move, girls!

It's difficult to see how this mattress-hopper pattern is much different from revolving-door marriages. Of course, it's a lot easier to duck out of a live-in situation —no lawyers, no alimony, and, alas, no sense of responsibility. But there may be just as many tears and broken hearts.

3 | Pinpointing the puzzlement

Why is it so hard to tell the difference between a real love and mere romantic infatuation? Why does this problem leave so many people perplexed?

All of us must ask ourselves a tough question: Will my marriage turn out to be a success—or a sad statistic? Chances are that you will not be able to detect real love, if and when you find it. But why not?

The tragic truth is that your culture—past and present—has just plain failed you. In our Western society we tend to put much stress on the place of love in marriage. Yet, for the most part, you have been denied the proper tools to help you recognize what real love is. Some of the things we call "love" have been with us for ages. Let's look at a few examples.

There was confusion then . . .

In the 12th century B.C., Israel's King David became lustfully enamored of Bathsheba as he watched her bathe. She was the wife of one of his soldiers who happened to be out of town at that time. David promptly proceeded to take her off to his own bed. (No kicking or screaming on her part is reported.)

Then there was the famed undying love of the old Hebrew prophet Hosea for his faithless wife Gomer. She had left his bed and board to become a harlot. That sad saga took place some 2700 years ago.

Medieval married women at times had highly romantic affairs with men other than their own husbands. Sometimes they let their "lovers" undress them completely and lie with them in bed, bare as Mother Hubbard's cupboard. But it was well understood that there was to be strictly no hanky pank! Intercourse was clearly a no-no. It was never to be a part of such romantic encounters. At least that's the story that got passed down to us.[1]

From these brief snatches of history we can readily see that the word "love" has been used to describe all kinds of quite different things. Compare the patient devotion Hosea had for his undeserving wife to the "lust at first sight" feelings displayed by King David.

There's a world of difference between the two, isn't there? To use the single word "love" to describe such diverse human emotions has to be troublesome.

. . . And confusion now

The meaning of "love" is still being much confused. It may be even worse now than it used to be. Although most Americans want a marriage based on love, society has failed to help us detect love. That failure has contributed to our high rates of divorce and loss of faith in marriage.

Yet each time you get those stars in your eyes, you

will need to decide if it's real love. Unless you can do that, and do it better than most people have in the past, you too will be stuck with those frightful heads-or-tails odds. And that is too chancy a choice. You deserve a better break.

Not only do most of us want love, we need it as well. The slogan "even dirty old men need love" expresses a truth. So do dirty old women and dirty little kids. Each of us needs at least one other person who really cares about us. We need someone who shares our hopes and joys, our sorrows and concerns. We need someone who honestly wants us to be our whole selves, to be fully fulfilled. We want someone to cry when we die—and really mean it.

We also need to *give* love. We need to have some other person on whom we can lavish our own caring and sharing.

This human need for love and companionship helps explain why youths in every generation cling doggedly to the hope of finding some loving and lovable life mate. Despite the current frightening odds against marital success, we sense that life yields its maximum meaning and its finest fulfillment with a true love mate. We yearn to find someone with whom we can share the depths of our inner being. You can find that kind of love in a good marriage.

This is the American marriage dream. It seems so right to most of us. Why then does it often go so wrong? The blame lies in part at least on the failure of our culture to help us distinguish true love from false love.

It is bad enough that society has not come up with adequate answers on mate choice. But it has done even worse than that. It has dished out false and misleading views of what love is and how it can be detected. It has done more to confuse the issue than to clarify it. The results have been marital chaos.

Muddle in the media

No themes are more popular in the public media than love and sex. Clever ad writers know that love and sex are among our deep desires and needs, so they exploit these to the hilt. They use sex to sell us soap and soup and salt and sugar—everything from gentle laxatives to zingy soda pop. Near nudes in a host of suggestive poses are dragged in quick succession across our field of awareness.

TV soap operas are literally littered with "romantic love." Mary loves John, who loves his file clerk, who's in love with her doctor, who loves—of all people—his wife. Many movies and books center around love stories. And what about popular songs? Does any other word appear in the titles and lyrics half as often as "love"? Young and old alike are bombarded from morn 'til night with love, love, and more love. Why then doesn't every single one of us know precisely and without fail what love is?

That answer is not hard to find. These media have simply deceived us. They use the term "love" a great deal, but they are almost always referring to romantic infatuation. They're not talking about love at all! As a result, few know what love really is.

What is supposed to happen when the time comes for you to wed? Somehow, just out of the clear blue, you're suddenly supposed to be able to ignore all the romantic rot you've been spoon-fed for years. By some miracle of magic you're supposed to know what love really is and come up with a good mate.

The wonder is not that so many of our marriages fail, but that so many manage somehow to survive.

Unmasking the media myth

What is this false product that the media is always trying to peddle? The pattern of "media love" follows a fairly set sequence.

They meet, lights flash, they fall helplessly and hopelessly in love. Obstacles arise, but all barriers fall in the face of their great and marvelous love. Finally, they marry and live happily ever after.

But hold on just a minute. That last phrase sounds strangely familiar. Isn't that the way *fairy tales* are supposed to end? You bet it is. And that's exactly what the romantic media myth is—a great big fairy tale. Sad to say, that suggested scenario seldom works out in real life. The actual path of "romantic love" tends to be quite different.

Wendell Johnson years ago called romantic love the "IFD disease." First, the other person is *Idealized*, and so is the situation the couple find themselves in. Since the ideals they dream about cannot become real, this brings on *Frustration*. That leads in turn to a loss of heart and morale, which then ends in *Despair*.[2] That's a far cry from what the media myth dream is supposed to be like.

Failure of religion

Our Judeo-Christian heritage has, like the media, let us down regarding the nature of love. Religion has not made clear to us love's multiple meanings. The problem goes back to the Hebrew and Greek languages in which the Old and New Testaments were recorded.

42

In *Sex and Love in the Bible*, William Cole makes this important point:

> The Old Testament uses the same word, *aheb* . . . to denote the love of God and the love of man. A similar economy of words prevails in the realm of human love, where the one verb and its [derivatives] refer not only to man's love for God but also his love for neighbor, including sensual love for members of the opposite sex.[3]

Now, that's a wide span of meanings for just one small four-letter word. If that one word had all those meanings, how were even the translators to know in each case which kind of love the writers were talking about?

Now what about the New Testament? It's track record on clarifying love seems no better, but here the problem is just reversed. The confusion is not, as in the Old Testament, that one root word means many things. The problem is rather that a number of Greek words, each of which had its own unique shades of meaning, were at times all translated into the English as simply "love." That is, those many Greek meanings were all lumped together into just one English word.

Those many shades of different meanings served a very useful purpose for the Greeks. They helped the Greeks to sort out just what kind of love was under discussion. Such shades of meaning also must be a great help to the Greek scholars of today. But our Bible translators gave us no such wealth of words and meanings. All we can do is try our best to guess which kind of love the Bible writers had in mind each time the word is used.

Let's take a brief look at each of the five Greek words for "love."

1. Sensual love. This is sexual desire. Greeks called it *epithymia*.

2. Yearning for unity. This meant for the Greeks a drive to unite with something attractive. They called it *eros*. Our English word "erotic" means passion and sex, but for the Greeks, *eros* had a much broader meaning. It could even be used to describe love for God. C.S. Lewis uses the word to mean "falling in love." [4]

3. Brotherly love. This is the kind of love shared by good friends and companions. It is a close feeling that develops when two persons have many things in common. The Greek word for this was *philia*.

4. Family affection. This is the kind of love shared by parents and children. The Greeks called this *storge*.

5. Self-giving love. The Greeks called this *agape*. Early Christians associated this type of love with Jesus. It is the self-giving devotion to others regardless of their merits. There are some people you don't think are very lovable, but you can love them anyway, simply because they are human beings.

Guessing at meanings

Clearly, each one of these five words used by the Greeks has its own distinct meaning. Each is quite different from all the rest. Yet Bible scholars translate all five of them into the one English word "love," giving us no clue as to the original thought. Bible readers who don't know Greek are left with a hopeless task. Each time we come upon the word "love," we must try to figure out the content from the context.

In this sense, then, our religion has indeed failed us. Obscurity in the Scriptures and muddle in the media leave us confused as to what love is all about. Is love sexual attraction or friendly fondness or brotherly affection?

When all these meanings get loaded onto just one word, the result is confusion. No wonder we have a hard time deciding when we've found true love.

Real love includes all five

A good marriage will likely need to have every one of these five types of love—and have them in healthy helpings.

1. Strong sex interest. Hornell Hart used to tell his classes at Duke that three things had to be true for the human race to survive. We had to (a) get our breakfast, (b) avoid being someone else's breakfast, and (c) have at least a passing interest in sex.

Well, for most of us, interest in sex is a trifle more than passing. Couples normally have strong erotic feelings for each other. A good marriage includes mutual joy and satisfaction in sex.

Yet it is quite possible to give sex an importance far beyond what it deserves. As a youth, I was told by a Ph.D. from Yale that "good sex is 85% of a good marriage." That was and still is utter nonsense. Any Ph.D., and certainly one from Yale, should know better. Sex is important, but it is only one of many important parts of a good relationship.

2. Respect and admiration. Couples need to have a strong mutual attraction and hold each other in high regard.

3. Friendship and fellowship. Couples also need to be true comrades. They need to have many things in common—the more the better. They must like each other a lot.

4. Affection. And, of course, there must be affection.

45

Each partner should provide the other with a haven of refuge from harsh attacks in the outside world. We all need sympathy and empathy to soothe our hurts. We need to be understood. Love can mean a shoulder to cry on when our burdens are too heavy to bear alone.

5. Self-giving devotion. Finally, a good marriage has to have a good deal of *agape* love. All of us have some unlovable traits. A spouse must at times love not because of, but in spite of, the other person's faults. You will have to love your mate even during those times when you feel he or she does not deserve it. Like you, your spouse may sometimes not be very lovable. That will take some *agape*.

A good marriage will have a heavy sprinkling of every one of these kinds of love. More than that, no one of them (with the possible exception of friendship) is enough in itself to build and sustain a healthy marriage. A balance of all five is a better bet.

The failure of social science—
a professional pussyfoot

We might well expect that the social sciences would be of most help with this problem of love. Researchers have made many kinds of studies about dating and mating over the years. Since the number one courtship query of youth is "How can I know if it's love?" isn't it logical to assume that this issue should have had prime time with the social researchers? It may seem logical, but it doesn't happen to be true.

From the "brains": disdain

The hard fact is that in this century there has been only one book which gives full treatment to this subject: *Of Love and Lust* by Theodor Reik.[5] And even this excellent book has some serious drawbacks. It has more than 600 pages, which would discourage many young readers, and it is full of technical terms. With the dearth of useful data on love, no wonder so many people are confused about how to detect the real thing. We social scientists have failed to cope with this critical need. Like religion and the media, science has largely failed to help you recognize love.

Compounding the confusion: certain symptoms seem similar

One further factor makes it hard for you to know if you're really in love. Many of the same romantic symptoms occur in *both* love and infatuation. It's important for you to know what these similar symptoms are.

Powerful pull to passion. You may think that if you have strong sexual feelings toward another person, you must surely be in love. That is far from the truth. Sex attraction can exist without love. Indeed, you may feel passionate toward a person you've not met. Their picture, their appearance on the stage or on the screen or mere daydreams may be quite enough to arouse your sex interest.

If you like a member of the opposite sex well enough to want to be with them a lot, don't be surprised if you feel a good deal of sex interest too. If you engage in a lot of necking and petting, sex feelings may become highly urgent. Sex may even become the most prominent part of your relationship. But even that kind of desire does not mean your love is real. Sexual urges can be just as strong in false love as in true love.

Gnawing need for nearness. As it is with sex interest, so it is with the deep desire to be together. It can be present in infatuation just as in love. You may want to be together almost all the time. If you are parted for even a few hours you will have a feeling of emptiness, a deep longing for each other. Does this mean you have real love in your relationship? Not at all. Such longing can be as much present in false love as it is in the real thing.

Funny feelings. Getting strange feelings "in the middle" when you see or think about another person is not in itself a valid clue. That happens in pseudo-love every bit as much as it does in real love.

You may feel like you're walking on clouds. As long as things go well between you, your joy knows no bounds. That you "have each other" is quite enough—nothing else seems to matter.

But when things go wrong between you, your misery is equally strong. You have a hollow feeling in the pit of your stomach. You long for things to be right again between you. Your pride may not let you show your feelings openly, but you'd give almost anything if you two could again be the same as you were before.

So that must mean you love each other very much, right? Dead wrong. It can happen just like that in infatuation, every bit as much as if it is love. Such feelings are perhaps even more likely in infatuation.

Pull to passion, need for nearness, and funny feelings—these three clues are romantic fool's gold. Like a greenhorn prospector, you may get all excited in the firm belief that you've struck it rich. But the greenhorn prospector mistook pyrite for gold, and you may mistake infatuation for true love. You may have strong sex feelings, a need for nearness, and a host of strange new emotions. But don't trust such clues. They may be romantic fool's gold.

To detect Pyrite there is one simple test. Just pop it into a pan and put it on a hot stove. If it's real gold, it won't be damaged. But fool's gold will sizzle and smoke and send out a strong stench. Sad to say, there's no such simple test to detect romantic fool's gold. You can scarcely put your love in a hot pan—at least not for very long!

All of this may lead you to conclude that no help is to be had with this problem. That is not true. But you do need to keep two things clearly in mind. First, look for more valid clues than the three described above. Second, go slowly.

WANTED: A love that lasts

All of this is indeed discouraging. It is almost as if your culture has conspired against you. It has laid down rigid rules defining high goals for marriage success. Then it has built road blocks which tend to keep you from reaching those goals. Yet the awful fact remains—you must try to predict in advance whether your choice of a mate will be a wise one. It is one of the most important decisions you will ever have to make.

It is no wonder that thoughtful young people become anxious about this choice. But don't despair—you *can* determine whether it's real love or a mere infatuation. Science can help.

There are 14 simple clues you can use to test a relationship. Taken together, these clues will tell you whether it's genuine love. Furthermore, you can easily use 13 of these clues in your own situation, and you can do it all by yourself—during the romance.

Just ask yourself each of the 14 key questions which appear in the following chapters.[6] Then carefully think

49

about how the traits for each of these clues seem to apply to your specific case. Finally, based on an honest, unbiased assessment of the total results, determine the degree to which real love seems to be indicated for your romance.

Three precautions

Before you look at the 14 clues, please note three things:

1. *The order is not important.* Just because a clue comes early in the list, you should not assume it is of more value than clues listed later. It is not. The clues are not arranged from high to low, or low to high.

2. *No clue can stand alone.* No one of the clues is of itself a sound basis on which to make a decision. It would be a big mistake to act rashly.

One young woman, soon after hearing the 14 points explained in class, came by the teacher's office. "Prof," she announced, "I broke up with my boyfriend last night."

"You did? Why was that?" he asked.

"Well number seven hit us right between the eyes!"

Well, maybe it did. But just because one or two of the clues seem to point to romantic infatuation instead of love, that is no cause to call it quits. That would be a gross misuse of the 14 clues.

There may well be no such thing as "pure love" or "pure infatuation." Your relationship is much more likely to be a mixture of both. So you need to look beyond what is indicated by any one clue. You need to find out what the whole pattern of all the clues seems to show.

Ask yourself: "Into which category do *most* of the traits in this relationship seem to fall?" Can you honestly say that a high majority of the 14 clues do indeed fall into the real love column? If not, you can assume that you don't yet have enough love to consider marriage. Give your relationship more time, then test it again with the clues. See if it grows into love as time goes by. To qualify as a reasonably valid love, you need good scores on at least 10 or 11 of the 14 clues. Anything less would be a flimsy foundation for marriage.

3. *One-sided loves won't work.* Love must be mutual. No matter how solid you feel your own love is, the other person must love you in return. Otherwise, there is bound to be trouble ahead.

A young woman once admitted to me that she knew her young man didn't really love her. Yet she kept pressing him to marry her. "Just give us a year of marriage and I'll make him love me," she declared. She'd better not count on that. Most people are pretty much the same after marriage as before. There's no magic in a marriage license.

4 What is the major attraction?

What is your main interest in the other person? What appeals to you most? Your answers to these questions can help you decide if it's love.

Signs of infatuation

If you are infatuated, *your main interest is likely to be the person's physical equipment.* For males, that probably translates into whether the woman has a pretty face and nice curves in all the right places. A pair of manly shoulders may really get a female's attention. When girls sigh, "Gee, he's cute," or boys exclaim, "Wow! Get a load of that!" they don't exactly mean that the other person has a bright brain, do they?

All of that suggests infatuation. The main stress is on things you can perceive right away—what you can see, hear, smell, taste, or touch.

Signs of love

If you truly love someone, on the other hand, *your interest is in his or her total personality.* You're attracted to the whole person. The physical features are only some of the many things you like. It's not just the body you care about, it's what's housed *in* the body. It's not just what shows on the surface, but also what's beneath the surface. The face after all is just a mask. It's what's behind the mask that counts most. Real love arms you with X-ray vision—you can see far more about the one you love than what first meets the eye. And that's all to the good.

Young people today have a great way of making this point. They say, "You're a beautiful person." Now, they don't mean by that that you'd win a beauty contest. You may have a face that would stop a clock! What they mean is that you're a beautiful *kind* of person—nice to be around. Whether or not you *look* beautiful, you *are* beautiful.

You'll want to keep this distinction clearly in mind in the search for love. Some men make a tragic mistake —they pass up a beautiful woman to marry a pretty girl. But looks can be deceiving. A beautiful face and a handsome body are like the wrapping around a gift. The outside glitter tells you nothing at all about what's inside. Any old thing can be done up in a nice wrapping, yet the contents may be something you won't like at all. In fact, a gift box may be completely empty—and so may a pretty head!

Out of the dozens of high school assemblies I went to as a boy, I recall only one. "Boys," the speaker said solemnly, "before you marry a girl for her pretty face and sexy form, ask yourself: What's she going to look like in 30 years?" That stopped me.

Indeed, what *will* she/he look like in 30 years? She'll no doubt have her share of wrinkles and unsightly sags and bags. He may sport a shiny bald pate where that lush crop of curls now hangs. And his Greek-god chest? It may well have slipped down a foot or so. Probably neither of you will look like too much by then. In spite of that, you'll be expected to remain married. If you're to do that, you'll need more going for you than a few faded memories of how pretty or how handsome each of you *used* to look.

What if you marry for sex?

Strong physical attraction is normally tied to sex interest. But even if a couple's sex life is the very best, that isn't enough. A marriage based only on sex attraction will last no more than three to five years.

Consider a few solid facts of life before you marry for sex. For instance, do you know how often the typical American married couple has sex during an average week? The answer is two or three times (that's per week, not per night!) And do you know how long the average American married couple spends in sexual intercourse each time? It's just eight minutes—and that includes foreplay and afterglow! They spend only four to five minutes in actual penetration.[1]

Some say these numbers are a sad commentary on American sex life. Be that as it may, it's clear that we devote very little time to sex. Let's add up the total. (We'll take the larger figure. We don't want anyone to feel cheated.)

Number of times per week   3
Number of minutes per time 8

Grand total   24 minutes per week

There are 168 hours in a week—and the average couple spends less than half an hour of that time having sex! *Question:* If you marry mainly for sex, what in the world are you going to do the rest of the time? Why, you're going to spend more time looking at each other across the breakfast table (curlers, whiskers, and all) than you'll spend copulating in bed. So you'd just better have something worthwhile to talk about. No matter how torrid that half hour of sex might be, life can get mighty dull the rest of the time.

Some erotic interest in members of the opposite sex is of course to be expected. The story goes that an aging Supreme Court justice once spotted a sweet, young thing undulating down the walk. He stared for a few moments, with never the slightest show of shame. Turning to an aide he sighed, "Ah! Would that I were a man of 60 again!" The old codger may have been aging in body, but he had some pretty young ideas.

It's quite normal for us to feel physical attraction, be it in the context of love or infatuation or just that fleeting "instant urge." The key is how much importance such feelings have in a total relationship. In infatuation, the other's body is the *major* interest. In love, it is but one of many elements that attract.

5 How many factors attract?

How many things about the person attract you? Your answer can help you know whether your feelings are real love.

Think of as many things as you can that you really like about him or her. Jot them down in a list. Include such things as the way a person acts, thinks, feels, and looks. What about life goals? Hobbies? Habits? Religion? Favorite interests? Motives and ambitions?

When the list is fairly complete, go through it and do three things. First, place a check beside just those things which you find *really* attractive about the person, traits that you very much like and admire.

Second, underline those factors which you and the other person share as interests. Do you think alike, feel the same, react pro and con to the same things? What things do you disagree on—even clash about? Draw a circle around those.

Finally, ask yourself *why* you are interested in those

shared attractions. Were you interested in them *before* you met him or her? If you took an interest in golf or skating only after you found your friend liked it, your interest may not be genuine and lasting.

Take for instance the matter of religion. Suppose one of you grew up Methodist, the other Roman Catholic. You both feel you want religion to play a vital part in your home. Let's say the Protestant is persuaded to switch rather than fight—so as to keep religious peace in the family. Does that mean the matter is all settled? Probably not.

The track record of such marriages is far from encouraging. Several studies show that Protestant-Catholic unions fail almost three times as often as marriages where partners have had the same faith.[1]

Ask this question: Would you adopt the other person's religion by your own choice even if you two were to break up? If the answer is no, you'd best beware. Interests you have or actions you take because of the other are not likely to last. Once married, you may lose your enthusiasm for such arrangements with frightening speed. On the other hand, interests that each of you had before you met are quite certain to stay with you, together or not.

Signs of infatuation

In an infatuation *the number of factors that attract you are relatively few.* He may be very much struck by her lovely hair, her pretty legs, her bubbly laugh. She is very fond of his nice smile, his teasing sense of humor, the way he walks. And that's about the size of it. Just a few things attract.

However, those few things that do attract may seem *very* enticing. He may think she has the softest hair he's ever run his fingers through. Her legs are the prettiest he's ever seen, her laugh is utterly delightful. His smile may just melt her heart, and his jaunty walk thrills her no end. She can't resist laughing at his clever quips and jokes. Some things about the other really "send" you.

Still, the truth remains—only a few things attract you to the person. But what about all those dozens of other personality traits the person has? Maybe you haven't really thought much about those. You've been preoccupied with the things you do find attractive. Can those other things, in your view, just wait until later? Do they seem unimportant? That means you're just infatuated.

Signs of love

If it's love, *many or most qualities of the person— and the relationship—attract you.* You like not only the way the person looks and talks, but the way he or she thinks and feels about things and other people. Do you like the person's reactions to personal success? To failure? To tough challenges? To faults in his or her self, and in you or others? What about use of leisure time? And what about thoughtfulness, kindness, courage, temper, and temperament? Does the person have healthy and balanced attitudes toward money, sex, school, family, and friends? Toward the past and the future? What about bad habits?

Each of us has a multitude of traits and emotions and ideas and attitudes. An individual personality has many different sides. So ask yourself two questions. (1) How many of the countless characteristics of this person do I know enough about? (2) How many of those things do I find attractive? If you don't know very much about the person, you can't judge the relationship. You need time and effort so you get to know him or her extremely well. Only then can you judge your reaction to the many, many facets of that person's nature. If many or most of those factors attract you, this tends to indicate real love. When the excitement and romance wear off in a marriage, you need lots of other interests in common to hold you together over the long pull. You need to *like* each other as well as *love* each other.

The interests you do have in common need to be important rather than trivial. It doesn't matter much that you like the same kind of pizzas and movies. It matters very much whether you agree on life-style and whether you want to have children, make lots of money, or have two separate careers. And do the interests you share depend on some special setting—a bowling alley, movie theater, dance hall, a high mountain? Or can you do most things that interest you anywhere and still enjoy each other?

Also consider how similar your backgrounds have been. Do the two of you come from the same type of family and social class? Do you have similar religions, political views, goals, and aspirations? The more things you have in common, the more likely you are to have the kind of foundation that can support the growth of real love.

Unexciting as it may sound, one of the best prospects for a good marriage is the boy or girl next door. You grow up with each other, play together as children, and go to school together. You get to know each other mighty well. And your family and social backgrounds are probably pretty much alike. That's all in your favor when it comes to adjusting to marriage.

Do opposites really attract?

Two persons who are psychological opposites may attract and have a good marriage. Social opposites almost never do.

For example, a person who has a psychological need to dominate other people may be quite happy with a mate who likes to be dominated. Their differences tend to complement each other and bring each of them psychic fulfillment. Their happy state will last, however, only as long as the less dominant partner is willing to submit. If he or she ever balks at such an arrangement, the marriage will be in trouble.

Though in some cases a couple may be psychological opposites and get along fine, social opposites are quite another matter. The greater the social differences, the greater the dangers. In fairy tales we read that a prince marries a scrub girl and they live happily ever after, but in real life it seldom happens. Make sure you are on the same social wavelengths before you commit yourselves to marry. Talk over a wide range of subjects and share ideas and backgrounds. Include things like:

- Social class
- Values and religion
- Children and birth control
- Money
- Where and how to live
- Concepts of marriage and role expectations
- Goals and hopes for the future

The more you agree on these and other key issues, the better your chances for success in marriage. You need to be friends as well as lovers. Too many opposites will *de*tract, not *at*tract. We all tend to like (and to like to be with) persons who agree with us on most things rather than those who do not. If you can share at many levels—ideas, activities, sentiments, goals—your marriage will wear well. If not, it will "wear out."

Can you rap and adapt?

No matter how compatible you are, your marriage will not be free of conflict. So your ability to adapt and adjust is of prime importance. Can the two of you work out differences? Can you talk over problems with honesty? Can you solve disputes without hurting each other? Do either of you get mad or get grumpy when things don't go your way? Do you feel free to share your true feelings, or do you hold back out of fear or lack of trust and confidence? You'd best find out *before* you marry.

It is not enough just to be able to communicate. Even couples who fight a lot are communicating. The essential thing is that you be able to work out together constructive solutions to problems, that you develop skills to work through conflict in creative ways. That gives you a great advantage when you have to face adjustments and make decisions in your marriage.

Doesn't familiarity breed contempt?

Folklore has long made this claim, but it's not true if a couple is well matched. If you two have few things in common and marry on the basis of surface attractions, then getting to know each other better may indeed lead to contempt. The more you know, the less you like each other.

But if you have many factors that attract and take time to know each other well before marriage, the opposite will be true. Then, as Zick Rubin suggests, "familiarity breeds *content*," not contempt.[2]

CLUE THREE

6 How did it start?

Think back to when it all began. Did you feel that you knew right away that "he (or she) is for me"? Or did your interest grow over a long period of time? How long did it take for your "love" to come into full bloom? Your answer to such questions can tell you a lot about whether your romance is real love.

Signs of infatuation

Infatuation *tends to start fast*. You know the story: eyes meet across a crowded room—and they know!

Well, bless their hearts! They don't know *anything*—except that they have a good first impression of each other. They like what appears on the surface. They are pleased by what they can discover about each other right away. They have a warm, glowing feeling of being "at home" in each other's presence. But no one can possibly know if it is real love on brief acquaintance.

What about "love at first sight"?

If there is one thing the science of marriage is quite clear about, it is this. There is no such thing as love at first sight.

A human personality is much too complex to permit instant insight. Your senses show you only the superficial, the shallow shell. Real love requires that you know and like the other person's whole self. You need to understand the full array of complex traits that lie hidden deep within the person. You are not going to discover all that through quick, casual contacts.

On top of that, you need to figure out whether those many facets of both your personalities will fit together well. You can't find that out in a few minutes, or even a few weeks. It will take months—maybe even years.

Signs of love

The evidence is clear. Love *starts slowly*. It can't be any other way. Studies have shown that the longer the period of courtship and engagement, the better the chances for success in the marriage. There is no substitute for time. A year is better than six months. Two years are better than one. Three years are better than two, four better than three, five better than four.

Do you exclaim in disbelief, "Five years!" Yes, five years. The statistics are crystal clear.

Obviously you can't afford to spend five years exploring many relationships. If you do, you may end up being decrepit before you marry. But you certainly won't need five years to find out that most of your relationships are not for keeps. With some it won't take you five minutes to make up your mind.

But take as much time as you need to decide wisely. The longer the courtship, the better your odds for a good marriage. Anything less than two years is chancy.

"But hold on a minute, Prof," someone says. "My Uncle Jehosephat and Aunt Citronella had a whirlwind courtship. They met, fell in love, and were married all in the space of two months. They've been hitched now for over 30 years and they're as happy as two bugs in a rug. Now what do you say to *that?*"

I say: "Thank God, they lucked out!" It just so happened that they did have the seeds of a good match. But in the space of only eight or nine weeks they could not possibly have known that. They took one whale of a gamble. In this case, they won—but the odds were strongly against them.

Of course, time is not the only factor. It depends in part on what you do with that time. Maybe you meet, then after a few days together are separated for a long time. Though four years pass from the first kiss to the wedding day, you may have actually been together only a few short weeks. That is not enough. That does not pass the test of time.

The quality of the time spent with each other is as important as the quantity. People can be great actors. We all tend to play games with one another, to appear to be what we are not. A couple might date for a long period, yet have a shallow knowledge of each other. You need to find out what the person is like way down deep inside, beneath the display-window mask.

For years I've made a bold suggestion to students: "No couple should marry until they've spent at least one weekend camping together—properly chaperoned, of course." You may learn more from one campout than you can from a dozen dates where each of you is on your best behavior. Find out how he or she reacts to a tough problem.

64

Suppose it rains in the night. Someone forgot to trench around her tent. Water seeps up through her sleeping bag. She starts to squirm in discomfort. She gets up cold, wet, and hungry. But the matches got wet, so no heat and no breakfast. Take a good, long look at how she acts then.

And how about if he slips and falls while fishing, banging his tailbone on a rock? He gets doused in ice cold water. He loses a big fish, and with it his favorite rod and reel. He comes in drenched and dripping. Look him over very closely.

Does she blame him for all her woes? Does he get mad and "cuss a blue streak" at his luck, or—worse yet—at her? Does she smolder and pout? Does he tease her when she's miserable, then grow angry when the ribbing is directed at him?

Or can they roll with the punches and see the humor in their sad situation? Can they laugh at themselves? The way you react to problems like these will be a good clue to how you'll react to tough problems in marriage.

The age of anxiety

Once you reach the late 20s the chances that you will marry within the next year grow less with each passing birthday. Many who reach this stage grow anxious. They may be tempted to marry just about anyone who comes along out of fear that they will not have a better offer.

One eager teacher on the verge of 30 met a young man at Duke summer school. After a whirlwind courtship of three weeks, they went to a nearby state and got married. It did not work out. It was a case of "marry in haste and repent in leisure."

You can feel very lonesome living alone, it's true. But you can also feel lonely and miserable living with your mate if you're not well matched. It's no fun to live with someone who doesn't understand and care for you. Better to stay single than to live in a marital hell.

When does it all start?

If you're young, extra caution is in order. Studies show that the young are more likely to be infatuated than genuinely in love. So the younger you are, the more time you ought to take to decide. A good, long period of courtship will help you be sure that it's the real thing.

7 | How consistent is your interest?

"The path of true love never runs smoothly." So goes an old American adage, and a lot of people take it at full face value. One couple even named their old car "Tru Luv"—since it, too, never ran smoothly.

Is this saying true? Or is it just one more example of how infatuation and love get all twisted around in the public mind? The degree to which a couple's interest in each other stays smooth and consistent can be a good clue to the nature of their romance.

Signs of infatuation

It is in fact infatuation rather than love that does not run smoothly. In an infatuation, a couple's *interest in each other comes and goes.*

If you are infatuated, your interest in the other will fluctuate. You are never quite sure one day how you will feel the next. Your interest may range from high peaks of certainty about your relationship and its future to deep valleys of doubt. One day you may feel sure this is the right person for you. You think you might just as well set the wedding date. Then you develop doubts. You wonder if the two of you should date others for a while, to test your feelings more. But then things go better again and you become more confident. Your feelings seem to bounce back and forth.

Feelings of uncertainty fit right in with what we've learned about romantic infatuation. If you're infatuated, you're attracted to only a few things about the other person—probably physical and surface traits. Your interest in each other grew rather fast. The roots of such a relationship are too thin to nourish it for long. The soil is too shallow to keep your interest in each other strong at all times, so your feelings are not consistent.

Sex may also be the reason for lack of consistent interest. If a couple becomes involved in pleasurable sex behavior, their interest in each other may vary more or less in direct proportion to the strength of their sex urge at any given time.

Signs of love

In real love *the relationship tends to even out*. It becomes more and more consistent. You can depend on your interest in each other staying pretty much the same over a long period of time. You feel comfortable with it, and with each other. If you don't reach the peaks of excitement so prevalent in infatuation, neither do you plunge to the depths. As time goes on, you come to count on your love. You know it will be there when you need it.

This is not to say that in real love there will be no problems to iron out, no hardships to work around in the early stages of your courtship. Any two people will find some rough edges to smooth out when they start to reveal and merge the many facets of their complex inner selves. Problems of adjustment cannot be avoided. But the longer you know each other, the easier it is to cope.

You will want to know with some certainty *before you marry* that the two of you have clearly achieved a close, happy, dependable degree of harmony and mutual fulfillment. The best way to predict the future is to study closely the evidence from the past and the experience of the present. If you had a good relationship all last week, and the week before that, and the month before that, then you are more likely to have it next week, and the month after that, and the year after that. The longer you've had a consistent pattern in the past, the more certain you can be that you'll have it in the future. Time takes a lot of the guesswork out of your big decision.

As real love grows, you stabilize your feelings and actions toward each other. You learn to resolve tensions between you. It becomes easier to talk over and work out your differences. As McCary says, "Mature love is evenly balanced and temperate. Where romantic love [infatuation] is hot, mature love is warm. Mature love is not an extreme, but a way of life." [1]

8 How does it affect your personality?

The common belief is that when you "fall in love" you don't act at all like your normal self. You lose your appetite. You can't sleep. You forget things, neglect things, drop things, foul up things. You're moody. You daydream. You stumble over chairs and stairs.

Can this really be love? Is love a state of being beyond reason and self-control?

Signs of infatuation

It is romantic infatuation, not love, which has *a disorganizing and destuctive effect on your personality*. Infatuation makes you less effective, less efficient, less your real self. People probably notice it right away.

"What's come over that kid?" Dad may explode. "She won't eat. She doesn't do her homework. She doesn't even hear when I talk to her. Is she sick?"

"Oh, no," Mom says with a smile. "She's in love."

She isn't either. She's just infatuated.

But Mom is scarcely alone in making this wrong assumption. Here, for example, is an excerpt from an article published in *Harper's Bazaar*.

> If you suddenly can't add up (when you always had straight A's in math) . . . or stand up on the ski slopes without his arm around you (although you were educated at [Aspen]) or shut up talking to him long distance—you're in love.[1]

Does that sound silly? It's a pretty good description of romantic infatuation. The sad thing is that the article calls the condition "love," thus plunging headlong into the media myth trap.

Walking around in a daydream may seem quite harmless. But some of the results of infatuation are not so innocent. Kelly notes that "immature love (infatuation) . . . is irresponsible and fails to consider the future consequences of today's actions."[2] In such a condition, you might well lose your head and do things you wouldn't otherwise think of doing.

Reik cites the case of a girl who sought counseling. "I did not consider any more whether it was wrong or right to kiss him good night," she said. "It did not matter, nothing matters any more."[3] If you let yourself get so involved with someone that "nothing matters" except your romance, you could be exploited and deeply hurt. The risk is especially high if the feelings of love or infatuation are mainly on one side.

The principle of least interest

One-sided love or infatuation occurs quite often. Scientists who study this condition have come up with what they call the "principle of least interest." This principle states that in a one-sided romance, the partner who has the least interest in the affair is able to control the other person. That's because the one who is more involved has more at stake.

No one should use another human being for selfish purposes, but some people do it. A girl who doesn't care much for a boy may keep him dangling on the string. It may build up her ego to have someone care so much for her. Or he may be just a convenience—she can always count on him for a date if nobody else asks her. She knows he'll put up with shabby treatment because he's so emotionally involved. It's a mean trick, but some girls do it.

If the boy is the one with the least interest in continuing the affair, he may demand more sexual favors than his girl friend wants to give. Since she fears he may leave her if she doesn't give in, she may yield just to try to hold him. Since he doesn't care very much for her, he may take advantage of her.

If a girl has to give a guy sex to keep him, she can well ask herself if such a fellow is worth keeping. If his main interest in her is sex, he'll probably drop her after a while anyway. On the other hand, if a boy really does love a girl, he won't press her to do things that he knows are contrary to her principles. He'll respect her right to do what she feels she ought to do.

Real love is responsible and glad to assume the consequences of mutual acts. Infatuation, on the other hand, tends to dodge responsibility. So when a boy says to a girl, "If you loved me, you'd let me," her logical reply will be, "If you loved me, you wouldn't ask me to."

Signs of love

Real love will have *an organizing and a constructive effect on your personality*. It brings out the best in

72

you. As Hirning says, "There is an intense and satisfying feeling of greater self-realization and expression, as well as a feeling of having one's own personality reinforced and strengthened and enriched." Duvall adds that love gives you "new energy and ambition, and more interest in life. . . . It is creative, brings an eagerness to grow, to improve, to work for worthy purposes and ideals. Love is associated with feelings of self-confidence, trust and security." [4]

The person who loves makes an effort to be more deserving of the beloved. Two sisters were heard to agree that their older brother's wife is good for him. "Before he met Jane, he had few goals and not much direction in his life," said one. The other nodded. "When he married her, it really made a man out of him." Love gave him the will to improve himself. Love lifted him to new levels of maturity and responsible action. It will do the same for you.

If you love someone, you want your beloved to be proud of you, so you try harder. Life has more purpose. You make plans and save for the future. Life takes on new meaning, more sparkle. You may daydream a lot, but your thoughts center on plans that are not beyond your reach. And you have more energy. Love woos you to function at your highest level.

Here's a good test for students. If you're infatuated, your grades will go down. If you're in love, your grades will go up. You'll be better organized and more alert. (You may study less but enjoy it more.)

Your friends and teachers and parents may well notice the change for the good. They may comment, "My, since she's been going with him, she takes herself and her duties a lot more seriously." Or, "Have you noticed how much more dependable he's become?"

If you experience real love, you may find that your attitude toward all people and the whole of life has been elevated. "We have heard 'all the world loves a lover,'" notes Duvall. "The converse is also true, 'Lovers love all the world.'"[5] Love doesn't make you turn inward and isolate yourself and your beloved. On the contrary, as Judson T. Landis notes:

> The man or woman who loves and is loved and accepted by one person can live and function in other relationships more effectively. He is free to be himself without defensiveness; he can worry less about protecting his ego from hurt. He can be more outgoing and confident in his relationships. People who love and are loved are not completely absorbed with love; they are more fully functioning personalities in all aspects of life. . . . It promotes growth and increases awareness of meanings, needs and opportunities in the world about one.[6]

What if you have loved and lost? You may have had a real love relationship that did not result in marriage. Perhaps one or both of you did not recognize at the time that it was real love. Or some tragedy may have robbed you of your beloved.

In spite of the pain of loss, you still are likely to be a better person for having had love. You can better understand yourself and be better prepared for finding success in your future relationships. You will be more mature. You grew through your love experience, and that growth will not all wither away. You will be more alert to find and hold some other love in the months and years to come.

Come what may, real love will have an organizing and constructive effect on your personality.

9 How and when does it end?

This clue has two parts: How long does the romance last from start to finish? And how long does it take you to get over it if it ends? Both parts are good indicators of whether it is love.

This is the only clue that can't be applied during the time the romance is in full swing. Naturally, you can't know how long it will last or how long it will take you to get over it if it hasn't stopped yet. This clue will nonetheless be of help to you as you look back on a past romance. It may ease your mind if you still have doubt about whether it was the real thing.

Signs of infatuation

If it is infatuation, *it stops the same way it starts— fast.* Some years back there was a TV series called "The Many Loves of Dobie Gillis." Young Dobie was "in love" with someone new every week. All of his "loves" were, of course, nothing but infatuations.

In the real world an infatuation may not end quite that fast. You may moon over his or her picture a few weekends before you start to get over it. But by and large an infatuation won't last long—*unless*.

That "unless" is very important, so capitalize it, underline it, italicize it in your mind. We'll come back to it in just a moment. First, let's note the effect of real love.

Signs of love

If it's love, *it stops slowly*. It cannot do otherwise. If you have come to deeply love another person, it's going to take you more than a few weekends to get over it if it ends. Love involves meshing many, many facets of two personalities. You grow together and become a unit. The person becomes a basic part of you, of your own personality. If a break comes, you're just not going to be the same. In fact, you may never quite get over it for as long as you live.

Have you noticed what sometimes happens when two old people have loved each other for many, many years? They become so much a part of each other that they often act alike. They may even come to look a lot alike. And what happens if one of them dies and all those close ties are suddenly severed? In so many cases the other one dies very soon, too. The dead partner had become so much a part of the survivor's life that the survivor feels lost alone and feels a deep longing to be reunited, even in death.

Young people can lose love, too. Does that mean that if you've lost your beloved you cannot love again? A lot of people used to think that. They believed firmly that there is just one person created for each of us to marry.

76

We know now that this notion is false. Social scientists are certain that there are a number of persons in this world with whom each of us normally can have a genuine, deep-seated love that will last. There are, no doubt, several of these within a short distance of your home base.

So if you've loved and lost, you have not been sentenced to being single the rest of your life. There is no such thing as a "one and only"—although after you're married it's a good plan not to keep looking over your shoulder at others. Once wed, just assume your mate is your one and only—for keeps.

Infatuations stop fast—*unless*

There is one major exception to the general rule that infatuations tend to break off early. An infatuation will end soon—*unless the couple becomes involved in mutually satisfying sexual relations.* If that happens, all bets are off on this clue. Sex will frustrate the usual test of time.

Don't cheat on the test of time

Usually, the longer a couple stays together and has a good relationship, the more certain they can be that it is real love. Why does this test not apply if they start to enjoy sex?

The answer is simple enough. They may stay together just for the sex, and not because they have a lot of things in common. They keep coming back for sex, not for the full companionship of meshing personalities. Thus they cheat on the test of time.

Studies indicate a good sexual relationship may hold a couple together as long as three to five years. But that's about it. Sex alone will not keep a couple together longer than that. So if they have no more in common than good sex, the relationship will wither away.

Good sex can fool you. A couple may think, "Well, the studies show that the longer a couple spends in courtship and engagement, the more likely it is that they've found real love. We've been going together three years now, so that must mean it's real love." Well, maybe so, maybe no. Three years together may mean that a relationship is good—but it may just mean that the sex life is good.

Since sex is so deceptive, this is one of the most important reasons to resist having sex early in a relationship. You need to be very sure that the rest of your relationship is on sound ground before you muddy up your emotions with sex.

If you don't wait, you've robbed yourself of one of the best of all safeguards to keep you from acting rashly on an unsound relationship. Is it worth it to forfeit this kind of protection against future disaster, just for the sake of a few present thrills and joys? Quite apart from the moral and religious issues or disapproval by parents and society, this fact alone seems reason enough to hold off on sex. You need the test of time working for you, not against you. Those who cheat on the test of time cheat no one but themselves.

"Making up" the test of time

"But we're already involved in satisfying sex relations," one couple told me. "We think we love each other, but we want to be quite sure before we marry. Is there any way we can still apply the test of time to our relationship?"

A lot of couples face this problem. There is a way out for those who really want an answer, but the remedy is not easy. As in any experiment in science, the variable—in this case, sex—must be isolated. That is, the relationship of the couple must be observed and tested *apart from* the sexual factor.

What the serious couple probably must do is arrange a rather lengthy separation, so they can't get at each other sexually for many weeks or even for a few months. They can stay in touch by mail and phone, but they must avoid all opportunities for sex. If their interest in each other survives the crisis of being apart that long, it's a pretty good sign that their interest involves love, not just sex alone.

"But," couples ask me, "why must we stay apart? Can't we just vow not to have sex for that same period of time, and go on seeing each other as usual?"

No. The reason is simple. Once a couple has established a habit of having sex, it is almost impossible for them to be together without it. One kiss leads to another. Like the alcoholic who sneaks one drink, they may find that they just can't stop. So a conscious choice to get away from each other for a fairly long time is the only way they can lay claim once more to that crucial test of time.

The decision to stay apart must be the couple's own. If parents or others try to force such a separation, the couple may just set their brakes and vow to ride out the test period. Then they rush back into each other's arms. The separation test won't work unless the couple themselves want to make it work. It's a bitter pill, but it's the only sure cure—and well worth the swallowing.

Let's pause now and look more closely at the whole question of premarital sex.

10 To be or not to be—a virgin

Whether to save sex for marriage is still a big question for most young people. The average youth is torn between strong arguments for it and against it.

On one hand, our society is dead set against you going all the way with sex unless you're married to your partner. This taboo is doubly strict if you're female. If that strikes you as being unfair, you're quite right. But a double standard does exist, and no girl or woman can safely ignore that fact. Fair or not, the double standard will no doubt continue to exist until science finds some way for boys to have babies. That may take a while.

In addition to strong pressures against premarital sex laid down by society at large, the main religious bodies in America strictly oppose sex outside of marriage. Parents, too, are nearly unanimous in opposing premarital sex—again, especially for females.

All these factors and more—risks of pregnancy, venereal disease (VD), etc.—should provide cause for pause for any serious young person. It takes a mighty strong person to fly in the face of harsh social pressures and get away with it. It's not likely that you are one of those rather rare exceptions.

On the other hand, the sex drive for the normal young person may at times be powerful and hard to control. Lures toward sex may be extremely urgent. Even the most strong-willed person may on occasion be sorely tempted to go all the way.

Also, the modern young person's peer group is probably much more tolerant of premarital sex. In the past, persons in one's own age group tended to show disapproval. That was an added nudge to hold the line. But today's youth are less quick to condemn premarital sex than their elders were. Many young people believe that what people do in their sex life is nobody's business but their own. That's not true, but some like to think it is.

Still other factors make it harder now for a young person to say no to premarital sex. Birth control devices are easy to obtain, and they are highly effective. If a couple "gets caught," it's easier to get an abortion. Most cases of VD can now be cured. And most couples find it easy to be alone, with no adults around.

So if we add it all up, the picture seems clear. Sex is now a pretty tough urge to resist. The view of some young people seems to be, "Why fight it?"

Isn't everybody doing it?

Not at all. Large numbers of single persons in the United States are virgins, though it is hard to know for sure just how many. Dozens of studies have been made, but their findings differ quite a lot. Some show that the amount of premarital sex is less now than before. Others suggest a sharp increase.[1]

The group who years ago did the Kinsey study doubts that there's been much change in U.S. sex habits in recent times. They claim the only sexual revolution in this country is what the mass media creates and promotes.[2] Some experts think Americans' sex behavior has not changed much in the last three generations and that youth today are just more open about it.

But even if the rate of premarital sex hasn't increased, it probably will in the near future. The youth of today are much more tolerant of such behavior.[3] It seems likely that those permissive attitudes will one day get put into action. A change in attitude tends to bring a change in behavior. But large numbers of young people are questioning these trends, and they want some straight answers. "What do *you* think about having sex before marriage?" they ask. That is one of the most frequent questions put to teachers and counselors.

Yet what kids really want to know is not so much what we think, but why we think it. Young people are not impressed by pious platitudes and mumbled moralizing. They demand honest answers based on proven facts. If premarital sex is wrong, they have to know the reasons. What they do about sex will have to be their decision. After all, when they're in the backseat of a car breathing hard, they're on their own. Mom and Dad and teachers and preachers can't help.

Over the years, when the issue of premarital sex has come up in class, I'd step to the blackboard, draw a line down the middle, and turn the question right back to the students. "OK, now *you tell me* whether premarital sex is smart or not. Give me all the arguments both for and against it that you've ever heard." Then I'd list the arguments on the board in two columns. When they were all there in front of us, we'd discuss each of them. If there were research studies that might apply to any point, pro or con, I laid those facts before the group. "Now make up your own mind," I would say.

A full list of arguments for and against premarital sex appears on pages 84–87. Groups of college and high school students over the past 15 years contributed to the list. I edited it just enough to weed out duplicate or out-of-date items.

The purpose of the list is to help you decide whether premarital sex makes sense. So mark your own answers and judge for yourself. How wise or unwise do *you* think it is? Be honest—and consistent.

After you've marked your checklist, we can consider what scientific studies have found. How does premarital sex affect your chances for a good marriage? Is sex before marriage a plus or a minus? Some of the findings may surprise you.

Nine known facts

Science has established nine facts concerning the probable effect of premarital sex on your marriage.

Fact 1. *Premarital sex tends to break up couples.* Other things being equal, couples who engage in sex are more likely to break up before marriage than those who do not.[4] So what about the young woman who gives in to sex in the hope that she won't lose her young man? She would more likely hold *him* if she holds *out*.

Fact 2. *Many men do not want to marry a woman*

83

CHECKLIST OF ARGUMENTS FOR AND AGAINST PREMARITAL SEXUAL INTERCOURSE

A. *Arguments offered for:* Indicate for each item the degree of soundness or unsoundness, in your judgment, of that argument for premarital intercourse.

	Very sound	Fairly sound	Unde-cided	Fairly unsound	Very unsound
1. It is the highest expression of human love.	___	___	___	___	___
2. It is the natural expression of sex.	___	___	___	___	___
3. It avoids frustrations aroused by petting.	___	___	___	___	___
4. It is a maturing experience.	___	___	___	___	___
5. A student cannot afford marriage.	___	___	___	___	___
6. It is a way a student can rebel if parents will not allow marriage.	___	___	___	___	___
7. It is a way to rebel against society.	___	___	___	___	___
8. It avoids responsibilities of marriage.	___	___	___	___	___
9. It is a method of getting a mate.	___	___	___	___	___
10. It brings pleasure, enjoyment, fulfillment.	___	___	___	___	___
11. It seems increasingly more sociably acceptable.	___	___	___	___	___
12. It is condoned by other modern cultures.	___	___	___	___	___
13. It satisfies curiosity.	___	___	___	___	___
14. It is a test of physical compatibility.	___	___	___	___	___
15. It is a test of mental compatibility.	___	___	___	___	___
16. It fills a need for affection (loneliness).	___	___	___	___	___
17. Why wait; the world may blow up tomorrow.	___	___	___	___	___

18. It's OK if you don't get discovered. |||
19. It can be used as an escape mechanism. |||
20. Some people have had experience living in a culture where premarital coitus was acceptable. |||
21. It is OK if done for fear of losing your desired mate. |||
22. Prohibitions inhibit expression of real love. |||
23. It is OK if the couple is engaged, planning marriage. |||
24. It is OK if they consider themselves married already. |||
25. Sexually experienced persons adjust more quickly to sex in marriage. |||
26. _____ |||
27. _____ |

TOTALS

B. Arguments offered against: Indicate for each item the degree of soundness or unsoundness which, in your judgment, that argument against premarital intercourse has.

	Very sound	Fairly sound	Unde-cided	Fairly unsound	Very unsound
1. The fear and danger of pregnancy.					
2. The danger of venereal disease.					
3. It causes guilt feelings.					
4. It brings social disapproval, pressure, penalties.					
5. The fear of being discovered.					

6. It violates religious beliefs.

7. A stigma is on the unwed mother and child.

8. Pregnancy is especially a problem if one is unable to accept marriage responsibilities.

9. May be forced to marry before it is wise.

10. It interrupts normal life patterns.

11. Its threat to the family as an institution.

12. Tends to prolong unsound relationships (infatuation) which normally would die except for sexual stimulation.

13. May lead to mental conflicts; in extreme cases, even mental illness or suicide.

14. Not likely to be as thrilling as anticipated due to abnormal conditions, fears, guilts.

15. Violates the ideal of chastity before marriage.

16. If you love your partner, you won't wish to expose him or her to probable negative consequences.

17. Abortions are dangerous, immoral, traumatic.

18. It tends to lead to crime or prostitution.

19. It tends to break up the couple before marriage.

20. It leads to doubts that your partner can be trusted.

21. It may lead to a pattern of fear, guilt connected with the sex act, even lasting into marriage.

22. It may impair the aesthetic (beautiful) aspect of sex in marriage.

23. Poor conditions for coitus usually prevail.
24. It tends to spoil relationships if pregnancy results.
25. If a child comes, it will likely be unwanted, and children *need* to be wanted.
26. Tends to lead to extramarital relations.
27. Causes loss of respect for self and sex partner.
28. Cheapens procreation, which is a sacred trust.
29. Many persons don't want to marry someone who has had intercourse with others.
30. Immaturity is reinforced—person wants the joy, pleasure of sex without any responsibilities.
31. The relationship may be exploitive, selfish.
32. Sexually experienced persons have less happy marriages.
33. Sexually experienced persons are more likely to divorce.
34. Sexually experienced persons are less happy with their married sex life.
35. _____
36. _____

TOTALS

Your Answer: In view of the above arguments both for and against, do *you* think sexual intercourse before marriage is wise? Check one:

____ Very Wise   ____ Wise   ____ Undecided   ____ Unwise   ____ Very Unwise *who has had intercourse with someone else.* Some fellows do their level best to reduce the number of virgins in the population. Yet when it comes time to marry, they don't want a girl who's been pawed over by other guys. Their strange logic seems to be: "It's OK for me to have sex with the girl *you* marry, but it's not OK for you to have sex with mine."

In the Kinsey study, about half the college-level males under age 25 expected to marry a virgin, or at least a woman who had had sex with no one else.[5] That proportion may since have changed, but many men still secretly hold that view.

Fact 3. *Those who have premarital sex tend to have less happy marriages.* On the whole, your chances of being happily married are better if you wait till you're wed to have sex. And the more premarital sex you have, the less likely you'll be happy in your marriage.[6]

Fact 4. *Those who have premarital sex are more likely to have their marriage end in divorce.* This follows from Fact 3. If a couple is unhappy with their marriage, they're more likely to get a divorce. And again, the more premarital sex the individuals have had, the greater the chance of divorce.[7]

Fact. 5. *Persons and couples who have had premarital sex are more likely to have extramarital affairs as well.* That is especially true of females. The Kinsey report shows that women who had sex before marriage were *more than twice* as likely to cheat on their husbands as women who were virgins at the time of their marriage. The more premarital sex a person has had, the more likely he or she is to commit adultery.[8]

This may well be the most serious consequence of all for a marriage. Few wives, and even fewer husbands, are able to tolerate—much less approve—acts of adultery on the part of their spouse. In some states a husband may even be held blameless for killing a man if he catches him in bed with his wife. But even in cases where it never gets discovered by the spouse, adultery may well drive a deep wedge between the couple.

Fact 6. *Having premarital sex may fool you into marrying a person who is not right for you.* As we have seen, sex can blind you. You may believe you've found real love, when in fact it is only sex which has held you together. If you wait for sex until you're very sure you have a sound relationship without sex, you can avoid this tragic error. Once your relationship is firmly established, then sex becomes a beautiful, wondrous bonus. It will tie you together even more completely in your marriage.

The next two facts are best taken together.

Fact 7. *Persons and couples with premarital sex experience seem to achieve sexual satisfaction sooner after they are married.* HOWEVER—

Fact. 8. *They are likely to be less satisfied overall with their sex life during marriage.* That is, they adjust to sex more quickly, but their overall adjustment is less satisfying than it is with couples who wait for sex until after they wed.

Learning to have good sex is in part a physical skill. In that sense it is like learning to play the piano or to ride a bicycle. You don't just sit down to the keyboard and rattle off a sonata by Mozart. Nor do you hop on a bike for the first time and sail off down the road. At first you make some mistakes. The more you practice any motor skill, the better you get at it.

Thus your first sexual experience is not likely to be all that great, especially if you're female. Both of you are bound to be a bit clumsy. It will take time for virgin newlyweds to get their sex life in order, no matter how much they love each other. But once they get the hang of it, their sex life tends to be happier than that of those who have experienced sex before marriage.

One reason sexually experienced persons may be less satisfied with their married sex life is that their premarital sex experience can rise to haunt them. Suppose that a certain wife has an orgasm about half the time when she and her husband have intercourse. She almost never has more than one climax during coitus. That is, in fact, well above the national average.[9] But what if the man she marries has had sex with other partners before? Isn't he likely to compare his wife's sexual "performance" with that of his previous partners?

People differ widely in their sexual nature and skills. Some are highly active, some are more reserved. What if in the past this man had sex with a woman who had several "whoopee" orgasms each time they had intercourse? This is not common, but it does happen. Will his memories of such experiences help or hinder his adjustment to sex with his wife? Will he be satisfied with his wife's more reserved response? Her responses are quite normal, yet he may feel cheated and unhappy.

Now suppose that this same sexually typical woman is married to a man who, like herself, has had sex with no one else. The only sex they have known is with each other. Are they not much more likely to be fully satisfied with the sex life they share? What they have is good, so they're happy with it. The statistics are clearly on their side.

Married sex is best

Almost any wife and husband can work out a happy sexual adjustment if they love each other. Any loving couple's sex life is likely to be just fine. When they have a warm, compatible relationship, they can with very few exceptions work out a good sex life. A recent *Redbook* magazine poll of tens of thousands of married men and women reveals that the vast majority are satisfied with their sex life together.[10]

Sex in the context of a meaningful, lasting relationship is by far the best. If you've never had sex with someone you truly love, you just don't know what sex is all about. Sex at only the physical level scarcely scratches the surface of deep meaning and true satisfaction. In fact, it's hardly even human. After all, any old dog or hog can perform pure sex. The purely physical concept of sex is quite beneath us as human persons. It's not worthy of our best selves.

Total sex

No matter how skilled and exotic and explosive a merely physical sexual experience may be, it cannot begin to match total sex. Total sex involves the completion and conjoining of total personalities. It merges the minds, the emotions, and the social and spiritual selves of a couple, as well as their two bodies. The two truly do become one.

Author Bill *(My Shadow Ran Fast)* Sands is an ex-con who made good. He hammered home this point about total sex to students at the University of Wisconsin-Platteville a few years ago. Some of the students were stunned by his words.

A young man asked Sands what he thought about having sex with others besides his wife. He replied,

"I see no point in it. Why should I settle for hamburger when I can have steak?"

It seems he had found a truly fine love, and with it a fine sex life. There's more to good sex than a breathless bounce in bed.

If you're engaged—why wait?

Couples who have avoided sex while dating are more likely to become sexually active once they're engaged. "After all," they reason, "we fully intend to marry. We're already publicly committed to each other, even if it's not yet in writing. If we take care to avoid being discovered and if we avert pregnancy, why wait?"

On the face of it, the arguments sound convincing. But what if you do get discovered? What if the woman does get pregnant? And what if you break up? One out of every three engagements in the United States is broken, and premarital sex is in itself one contributing factor.

Smart couples will not fail to consider these facts. But even if none of these things happen, there is one other grave danger that is overlooked far too often.

Premarital sexual experience may actually deprive you of much of the sexual joy you can and should have after you marry. By rushing into the joys of premarital sex, you may rob yourself of the deeper, more permanent joys of total sex. Fact 9 explains how and why this can occur. Unlike most of the facts we have discussed, this one applies as much or more severely to those who have had sex with nobody other than the one they marry.

Fact 9. *Poor premarital sexual habits can be carried over to spoil sex in marriage.* Sadly enough, this happens a lot. The Kinsey studies found that more than half of American wives are in some degree either not willing or not able to share sex freely and fully with their husbands. They have guilts and fears. They are hesitant or inhibited.

It's been a long time since the Kinsey research, and this high frequency may be lower now. Still, many wives—and to a lesser extent their husbands—have poor attitudes about sex.

Why is this so? A number of reasons are frequently cited. Our society still clings to some early Victorian prudery about sex. Then, too, many Christians have adopted St. Paul's view that sex is "of the flesh" and hence to be shunned. They believe it is at best something that is not quite nice. Then there has no doubt been poor sex education in home, church, and school. And unhealthy attitudes have been handed down by our elders. In all, Americans do have lots of "hang-up hangovers" from the past.

But in addition to these more familiar reasons for lack of sexual enjoyment is a factor that has escaped the attention it deserves. What is this culprit? It is *premarital intercourse*, along with other guilt-producing premarital sex acts.

Sexual salivation

I have labeled the process by which premarital sex spoils marital sex "sexual salivation." We all know about the famous experiment of Pavlov and his pooch. When shown food, the dog would salivate—its mouth would water. Each time the dog was shown food, Pavlov rang a bell. Soon the dog was trained (or conditioned) to salivate any time the bell rang, even when no food was in sight. The real *cause* of salivation—the food—was gone, yet when the bell was rung, the dog went right on salivating anyway.

So it is with premarital sex. Many sexual "hangups" in marriage have their roots in a similar process. Here's how "sexual salivation" works.

Since premarital sex is a social and religious no-no, illicit sex acts usually produce some degree of guilt, fear, and loss of self-esteem. This can apply to both partners, but it is especially true for women. They feel guilty, since they are doing what they believe they should not do. They lose self-respect, since they are not living up to their own ideals. And they are afraid of two things: getting caught in the act of sex, and becoming pregnant.

So what may happen if you get into a pattern of premarital sex? Whether you're engaged or not, each time you have sex, you "salivate"—you feel guilt and fear and loss of self-respect. Over and over again this happens. You have sex, you feel fear and guilt and remorse. In time, all of these negative feelings become associated with the sex act itself. As the dog came to associate food with the bell, you learn to tie sex with unhealthy feelings.

Now suppose you do get married. Once wed, you have no further need to feel guilt, fear, and remorse when you engage in sex. Once the relationship is made legal, you have social license to have just about any kind of sex you choose. So as soon as the ceremony is over, you will suddenly be able to forget all about the past—right? You can fall into your spouse's arms on the honeymoon and be utterly uninhibited—right? You will shed all that backlog of guilt, fear, and shame like a snake sheds its skin in summer—right?

Wrong! To the extent you learned to associate sex

with guilt and fear and shame before the wedding, to that same extent you will feel that way afterward.

Just as with the dog's food, the causes of the response have been removed. Still, every time you two "ring the bell" by having sex, that guilt and fear and shame will come back to haunt you. It may take months or even years for you to recondition yourselves. Only then can your sex life be full and free.

Small wonder so many husbands and wives are inhibited.

Consider the case of Jim and Mary. They have been happily married for many years. Mary had sex with no one but Jim before they married, but they did have sex with each other for about 18 months before the wedding. They were lucky. They got by without a premarital pregnancy, and they were never caught in the act of sex.

Did that mean they were home free? Hardly. Sexual salivation caught up with them. After 10 years and four children, Mary was still in some measure unable to give herself fully and freely in sex to her husband. Sad indeed.

Now Jim and Mary were not dummies. They had college degrees in sociology. Both became successful social workers. They had reliable information about sex and were alert to new insights in the field of married love.

But they also had a deep interest in religion. It was highly important to them to behave in ways they felt were right. So even though they got by without being discovered or without a premarital pregnancy, sexual salivation took a heavy toll. The price they paid was a dear one—the loss of a full, free sex experience through their early years of marriage. Is premarital sex really worth all that?

Illicit sex as forbidden fruit

The sexual salivation process before marriage may in part be responsible for extramarital sex—adultery—in later life. Indulging in "forbidden fruit" brings special pleasure and excitement. The watermelon swiped from the farmer's patch tastes far better than the one you buy from him.

Premarital sex is considered illicit, wrong. It is forbidden fruit—which may bring that special pleasure and excitement.

After marriage, sex is no longer forbidden. Couples accustomed to the excitement of forbidden fruit may find married sex to be dull. Might this tempt a spouse to try to find greater excitement outside the marriage bond—another kind of forbidden fruit?

Whether—plus how much and with whom

Let's sum up the nine known facts about sex before marriage. Other things being equal, if you have premarital sex you are more likely to:

1. Break up before you marry.
2. Scare off anyone who wants to marry a virgin.
3. Be less happy in your marriage.
4. Get a divorce.
5. Commit adultery after you marry.
6. Be fooled into marrying for the wrong reasons,.
7. Achieve married sex happiness quicker, *but*
8. Be less satisfied with your married sex life.
9. Spoil total sex due to sexual salivation.

It is not only significant *whether* you have premarital sex, but also *how much* you have. The more of it you have, the greater the impact of the nine facts on your marriage.

It also matters *with whom* you have premarital sex. If you have sex only with the person you marry, Facts 1 and 9 still apply to you, but for the most part the other seven facts apply less harshly than if you have sex with other persons as well.

But why not try out sex?

Some believe they need to test out sex before marriage. Since good sexual adjustment is important, they want to know beforehand what that part of their relationship is going to be like. "You wouldn't buy a car without first trying it out," a guy may say. "So why marry without trying out sex?"

This argument may sound logical, but it implies a highly unflattering view of a young woman. Like *Playboy* magazine, the guy sees a girl as a "plaything." She is a commodity to be acquired and used, not a life partner to be loved and cherished. That may be fine if he's shopping only for a sex object, but if he's looking for a permanent relationship it leaves much to be desired.

So a lot depends on what the "sex shopper" has in mind. Does he seriously intend to sign a contract, or is he looking just for the fun of it? A smart car salesman quickly spots the "joy ride only" customer. Once he does, he's not likely to allow that person any more trial runs with his merchandise. The smart young woman will do the same with the man who wants to "try her out" in bed. There are several reasons the "try it out first" idea won't hold water—even in a water bed!

The teacher and the plumber

Some people make one very big mistake. They assume that sex outside of marriage is going to be a valid sample of what sex will be like within marriage. But premarital sex is not a true test. Consider this case history.

A teacher in her late twenties and a young plumber become close friends. They had a great deal in common. The more time they spent with each other, the more they were certain that their love was real.

But they had one big problem. He said he could not agree to marry her unless they first tested out their sexual adjustment. To this she simply could not agree. She felt strongly that sex was only for marriage. To try it out beforehand, even with one she loved, went against her every belief and feeling. Yet he insisted. He just refused to marry otherwise. Finally, with great reluctance and deep feelings of guilt and fear, she agreed to submit to sex rather than lose her beloved.

Any good marriage counselor could guess how that experiment would turn out. Her nervous fears and guilts made her so inhibited and worried that the sex session was a dismal failure. Convinced that their sex life would never work out, he broke off the engagement, leaving her in a state of shock and deep depression.

How foolish for the man to assume from one premarital experiment that their whole married sex life would not be good! In the first place, the first sexual experience of any woman is not likely to be all that good—married or not. But if her first sex comes *after* she's married, the chances for success are far better. Once wed, she need feel no guilt, no fear, no remorse. She can relax and release herself to sex much more fully and freely. Premarital sex doesn't really give sex a fair trial.

It's not necessary to try sex first

If you have real love going for you, don't worry about your sex life being good. It will be. The exceptions to that rule are so rare that you can safely ignore the issue. If you truly love and respect your spouse, just relax. You will no doubt be able to work things out in your sex life. If that does not happen quite as soon as you think it should, read some good books or get some counseling to help you out. Mutual love and tender caring are far more important in sexual adjustment than are smooth techniques and wildly erotic responses. Above all, be relaxed and honest and considerate of each other. Nature will take care of the rest.

Sex Is Never an Emergency—that's the title of a recent book.[11] It suggests an essential point that's often overlooked. Sex is the only major human drive that does not have to be satisfied. You can't survive without eating and drinking, but the sex drive can be denied indefinitely. Sex may be important, but it's not crucial to the good life. A person can go a full lifetime without sex and suffer no serious damage. Priests and nuns have been proving that for centuries.

Girls report that some boys try to mislead them on this point. During an especially torrid "breathing hard" session, the boy may get highly aroused. Then his argument goes something like this: "Oh, Suzy, I'm too excited to stop. We've gone this far, you just have to let me go all the way. I'll just die if you don't let me. I've just gotta!"

Well, he doesn't "just gotta!" If he doesn't get to have intercourse right then, he's not going to break out in purple pimples! He won't suffer any permanent brain damage—or body damage either. It won't even stunt the poor boy's growth. He may have to run around the block a time or two before he goes home, but he can do that.

Then the next time those two had better call a halt to things before he gets so fired up. Some guys try to use force when they get that excited. That can lead to some pretty tense moments, and maybe lots of regrets.

What every girl needs to know

Girls are more likely than boys to be confused by these strong sexual feelings. Because of our society's double standard, there is a basic difference in what sex means to males and what it means to females. A man may want sex with just about anything that wears a skirt. He can enjoy sex with a pick-up or a prostitute, even though he feels no affection for her at all. But most women in our culture won't have sex with just any guy who happens to come along. For them, love and sex should go together. The typical woman won't agree to sex unless she believes she loves the man.

Unless a woman knows about this basic difference between females and males, she may be in for trouble. Say she goes out with a man she's very fond of. They park in a lonely spot. He comes on real strong with the sex bit. He seems to have international forelimbs— Russian hands and Roman fingers! His advances grow more and more urgent. She doesn't have to read a book to find out what's on his mind. He wants to have sex with her. Should she let him or not?

If she doesn't know the facts of life about guys, she may wrongly reason something like this: "I wouldn't want to have sex with a guy unless I loved him. Johnny clearly wants to have sex with me. That must mean he loves me."

Don't you believe it, Suzy! He may just be looking for a handy solution to his immediate problem. He might have just as much interest in any female who happens to be within reach. The idea of love may never have entered his hot little mind.

The tenderness trap

This situation can get even more complex. Suppose Johnny has been around enough to know all about this particular difference between females and males. He knows full well that women seldom agree to sex unless they think there is real love in the relationship. So what does Mr. Bright Boy do? You guessed it. If all else fails, he may resort to wild and ardent claims of undying love for her.

Now if she's smart, Suzy will be wary. She'd best not believe his claims of love unless his attitudes and actions support his words. Has he over a long period of time fully demonstrated that he really does love her? He's saying, "I love you very much," but maybe what he really means is, "I sure would like to score with you."

We hasten to say that many males have very high principles and would not be guilty of such deceit. But better for a woman to be safe than sorry.

11 | Keeping sex in its proper place

Do you hope some day to have a happy and lasting marriage? If so, you may want to "play the odds" by steering clear of premarital sex. As the "nine known facts" suggest, your chances for a good marriage seem far better if you wait for the wedding.

Yet your sex urge is still there. It won't "just go away"—and you don't want it to. You want to find some healthy way to cope with it. How can you stay sensitive to the sex urge, yet avoid going all the way? Where is it smart to stop? How far is too far?

From full repression to full expression

The many stages of sexual arousal form a spectrum ranging from one extreme to the other.[1] One extreme is full repression, complete denial of the sex urge. The other extreme is going all the way to intercourse. Starting with repression, each stage brings deeper sexual tension.

The road to arousal

	Necking	Light petting	Heavy petting	
FULL REPRESSION	Holding hands · Hugging · Casual kissing · Serious kissing	French kissing (?) · Breasts covered · Breasts bared	Genitals covered · Genitals bared · Oral sex (?) · Genital to genital	SEXUAL INTERCOURSE

Two of the stages are hard to place on the chart. French or deep kissing—what I call tongue-in-cheek kissing!—is by strict definition a last stage of necking. But its arousing effect on some may be so intense it could be classed as petting. Then again it may turn some people off completely. (Good grief—all those germs!) In like manner oral sex will likely have a negative effect on many people, especially women. It is largely a male invention anyway.

So how far should you go down the road to arousal? And once you've set a limit on how far to go, how can you hold the line? You must find the right answers for yourself, but here are five general principles which may help you decide what is best for you.

Principle 1. *Avoid the two extremes.* We have seen why it is hazardous to go all the way before marriage. The long-term risks hardly seem worth the sensual thrills of the moment.

But it is equally dangerous to take the opposite extreme and fully repress the sex urge. If you try to keep the lid on it by refusing to admit it's there, you're failing to deal with it intelligently.

A repressed desire does not die. It just gets pushed

out of the conscious mind and into the subconscious, where it smolders and festers, waiting its chance to be expressed in some hidden form. If you don't deal with it directly and consciously, it lurks in the shadows and gets distorted and dangerous. Note this example.

Jane was utterly ignorant about sex when she married John. In fact, when John kissed her once on a date she thought he had made her pregnant! During more than 25 years of marriage she saw sex as repulsive and dirty. She resisted all of John's normal advances. Several times she even tried to get doctors to prescribe that she should not have sex ever again.

Finally, as she approached menopause, I gave her a book aimed mainly at helping the inhibited wife.[2] Later, as she returned it, tears streamed down her cheeks. "Oh, if only I'd read this book 30 years ago," she sobbed. "It would have saved me a lifetime of hell!" She had so repressed her sexuality that she and her husband were robbed of the normal joys of married love.

In extreme cases, the sex urge may be denied so fully that it is in great measure destroyed. One law of biology is: Use it or lose it. Fish that live in caves with no light lose their sight. An arm that's never used will atrophy. A person confined to bed for many months must learn to walk all over again.

So it is with the sex urge. It is a fine and precious gift when used in the right way, but a potential source of tragedy when it is not. It would seem wise for young people to give the sex urge enough expression to keep it warm and alive for marriage, while avoiding the dangers of its misuse.

It is hard to say which extreme holds the harsher hazards—total expression or total repression of the sex urge. Both can ruin lives. That's why Principle 1 is: Avoid both extremes.

Principle 2. *Don't light more fires than you put out.* If your goal is avoiding the two extremes—full repression and full expression—the trick is to give the sex drive a healthy expression without going too far. But how far is far enough?

The answer to that question may depend on your age and maturity, your level of willpower, your ability to keep control of yourself and your situation at a given time. Can you say no to yourself and others—and mean it?

Deciding how far to go will also depend on how well you know and like the other person. How long have you been seeing a lot of each other? How much can you trust the other person—and yourself? Are you willing to accept full responsibility for everything you do?

No one rule of thumb will apply in every case to every person. We are all different. Some may find that they must stop at necking. Others may find they can go further with no real problems. You must determine for yourself how far down the road to arousal you can safely go.

But one principle would seem sound for all to follow. Express your warm emotions enough to keep them alive and healthy, but don't go so far that you're in even worse emotional shape when you stop than you were before. Don't arouse more passion than you satisfy, or you'll end up restless and frustrated and full of gnawing desire. If you're more disturbed and unhappy than you were to begin with, just what have you gained? Besides, you're probably skating on thin ice. Next time you may not be able to stop.

Principle 3. *Avoid all chance of pregnancy.* This may strike you as strange. If you're not going to have intercourse, why worry about pregnancy?

A virgin can conceive. It doesn't happen often, but it's possible. Some doctors report that they come upon such a case every few years. The woman has never had intercourse, yet she's pregnant.

How can that be? For a woman to get pregnant, a sperm must fertilize an ovum. So how can a sperm reach the egg without intercourse? Very simple. It enters from the outside.

A sperm has a head—to fertilize the ovum—and a tail. What's the tail for? Locomotion—just **Sperm** like in a tadpole. And sperm can swim around in any favorably moist substance. What is more, there are millions of them in every male ejaculation or discharge. Estimates of the number of live sperm in each male discharge range all the way from 2 million up to 500 million. Now that's a whale of a lot of little men—and every one of them has impregnating the female ovum as its sole goal.

If a couple engages in heavy petting and the male ejaculates, some of the discharge may be introduced to the moist surface of the female genitals—the vulva— via the fingers, or in genital to genital petting. If they've been petting heavily, her genitals are pretty sure to be moist.

Yes, you guessed it. Hundreds of live sperm may find their way right in through the opening of the vagina. Even if she has a hymen, there has to be some opening there or she couldn't menstruate. The sperm wriggle their way up in the vagina, in through the cervix and uterus, into the fallopian tubes, and wham! A virgin has conceived.

Hence, to avoid all chance of pregnancy, you must at the very least set your limit short of genital to genital petting. If you pet until the male reaches climax, take care that none of the ejaculate is introduced to the vulva or vagina.

A tale of two females

But is it all that bad for a young woman to get pregnant outside of marriage? Consider the responses of two young women who found themselves pregnant.

A young woman comes in with her husband. Both have had my course in marriage and they've come back to share some pleasant moments with "Prof." It's clear from the time they enter the room that they can hardly wait to break their news. "Prof, you'll never guess what's going to happen to us in August," she finally says—just as if nobody's ever had a baby before. They clasp hands, beaming. They are utterly delighted and proud that she is growing their very own baby in her womb. It is a joyous occasion for all concerned.

Now contrast that scene with a visit from an unwed female student. As she comes through the door, there's a dark cloud of gloom hanging over her head. "My God, Prof," she blurts out. "I'm going to have a baby! What am I going to do?" She clearly hates the fact that she's growing another little human being in her body. She's bitter and depressed and confused. Suicide has crossed her mind. She'd give anything in the world if she were not pregnant. What a contrast to the happiness of the married couple!

Well, what can this young woman do? There's no really good answer. But let's consider her options.

If the father is mature and responsible and if they love each other, they can get married. They will have dozens of problems, but it may work out. But what if they have little or no foundation of love? Forced marriages are highly unsuccessful. Marriage might create worse problems for all concerned—the innocent baby included. A shotgun wedding can kill a couple's chances for a happy life and bring misery to the child.

Abortion may be *an out* for some, but it may *be out* for others. It's out for Catholics and for others who believe that a new human being exists from the moment of conception. To them, it really would be murder—and that's a heavy load of guilt to carry for a whole lifetime. Moreover, unless it is done under proper conditions, abortion can be highly dangerous, even fatal.

She may have the baby outside of marriage, but then she has another difficult choice to make. If she gives the baby up for adoption, she will never see her child, never know who has it, never know if it's alive or dead. That may be best for her baby, but some women report that they continue to feel deep grief for years. Each time they see a child the right age, they wonder: Could that one be mine?

The other alternative is to keep her baby herself. Studies show that those who go this route score lower on maturity tests than those who choose adoption. And it can be a rough road. There is still a stigma placed on both the unwed mother and her child, especially in rural and small-town America. The woman's chances to marry are few. She may end up on welfare —at taxpayers' expense. Or her parents may have to help with the child's care and training. In all, the girl's dream of keeping her child may turn out to be a tragic nightmare.

So that's the tale of two females. The contrast is stark and sobering. No woman ought to have to face an unwanted pregnancy. But if a couple is risking pregnancy, they'd better figure out what they will do when it occurs.

So where should sex play be halted before marriage? Some place short of that point where the girl has even the slightest chance of conceiving a child. Fun is fine as long as it doesn't spoil something better.

In view of all this—plus the "nine known facts"—a lot of young people are concluding that sex before marriage just doesn't make good sense. It is *not* a disgrace to be a virgin. It is in fact pretty smart.

Principle 4. *Set your own limit—and stick to it.* Since it is your body, you have the right and the duty to decide what you do with it. It's a big decision. The stakes are high. Since you have only one body and one life to live, you'll want to claim the very most life can offer.

So when you decide what your limit will be, you'll want it to be a sound, sober choice. You'll want to think it through beforehand and not wait until you're breathing hard in a red-hot petting session. You'll want your mind to rule your emotions, not the other way around. Follow your head, not your passion. It's best to call a firm halt to the process before there's even the slightest risk that you might "lose your head"— and with it your virtue.

The toughest test comes once you're engaged. After you're fully committed to each other, it may be hard indeed to keep from going all the way. That's why I recommend long courtships but short engagements. That way it's not so hard to wait.

Some males expect the female to be the one who

109

puts the brakes on sex. But if you're a guy, you aren't excused from responsibility to set limits on your own sexual behavior. You have the duty to act responsibly just as much as the female has. If you want the woman you marry to be a virgin, you have no right to be other than virgin for her. The old double standard is as old-fashioned as the Model T.

Principle 5. *Couples who care, should share.* I'm a great believer in honesty in relationships. If you and another person come to care a great deal for each other, I think you should talk frankly about how far you will go in sharing sexual affection. If you care enough about each other to want to go beyond casual kissing, then you know each other well enough to be frank about your feelings.

So before things go very far, talk it all over in a serious, honest atmosphere. Let each other know how you feel. Decide together just where your limit is going to be. Then both of you should take equal responsibility for holding that line. If one of you threatens to lose control, then the other must call a halt. Why should it always be the female who has to say no? Isn't that a cop-out, guys?

But, alas, if the male is not man enough to assume his share of the burden, then the female must carry it all alone—fair or not. She's the one who will get pregnant.

12 | Some things you should know before you marry

In this day when a huge fund of scientific facts on sex can be found in any good library, there is no excuse for being ignorant. Let's quickly review how babies are made.

When a girl begins her menstruation or "periods," her body will produce from her ovaries one egg or ovum about once every 28 days. This ovum travels through the fallopian tubes to her uterus (womb).

If the ovum gets fertilized by joining a male sperm while in the tubes, it descends and starts to grow a baby in the blood-enriched wall of the uterus. If the ovum is not fertilized, it is dissolved and menstrual blood passes out of the cervix or neck of the uterus. It goes through the vagina and is discharged.

Male sperm are introduced into a woman's body through her vagina, the larger opening at the lower end of her vulva. The vulva is the visible portion of her genitals or female organs. It is located between her upper thighs and at the base of the trunk of her body. During intercourse the male inserts his erect penis into the woman's vagina and ejaculates or expels semen or fluid containing sperm at the opening of the uterus. The sperm then swim through the woman's cervix and uterus and into the fallopian tubes. There they sometimes meet and fertilize the ovum.

If a woman's vagina has not been penetrated by a penis or some other object, she may have a membrane of flesh called a hymen. This hymen covers part of the vaginal opening. When it is ruptured, it may be quite painful for her. In extreme cases a woman may have such a tough hymen that it will not break. It may then have to be clipped by a doctor before intercourse is possible. In other cases a woman may have no hymen at all.

Once the ovum is fertilized by a single male sperm, it starts to grow in her uterus. She is pregnant. The fetus grows in her lower abdomen for about nine months. Then the muscles of the uterus start to contract. They squeeze the baby through the cervix and out the opening of the vagina. This is called labor and birth. Another human being is thus brought into the world.

The "favored four" contraceptives

Many married couples choose to delay having children or decide they don't want any children at all. Once you marry, you and your spouse must make this decision. Unless you're prepared for immediate pregnancy, you need to know how to prevent it. Highly effective ways to prevent conception are now available. But none of them is perfect, and some may pose hazards to health.

The four contraceptive methods doctors and other experts commonly recommend are the pill, the IUD, the diaphragm with spermicidal jelly, and the condom. The first three are used by the female, and each of them requires the attention of a doctor to be safe and effective.

The contraceptive pill

The pill acts to control the chemistry of the woman's body. In effect, it fools her body into thinking she's already pregnant. She may even exhibit such symptoms as morning sickness. It must be taken each day without fail for a certain period—usually 20 days —then it is not taken for several days. The instructions should be followed to the letter.

The pill prevents the ovum from being expelled at the usual time—normally about 14 days before the onset of the woman's next period. When she stops taking the daily pill, she menstruates as usual and the cycle begins anew.

Women should never take birth control pills except under a doctor's care. Don't ever steal them out of mother's cupboard. They may kill you—literally. What is protection for one woman may be poison for another. Some women with special medical problems should never take the pill. For most it is safe, but some studies indicate a possible link with cancer in women who take the pill for many years.

The intrauterine device

The IUD is a small, wirelike gadget that is placed in the cervix. It comes in many forms—loops and spirals are common. It may be of metal or plastic, and is especially effective if there is copper in it. The "shield" type is not recommended for reasons of safety. All types must be inserted by a doctor.

The best theory about how the IUD works seems to be that sperm go right through to the tubes. But even if the egg is fertilized, it does not attach itself to the uterine wall and grow. Perhaps the IUD acts as a "foreign body" and causes rejection of the fertilized egg. This method is thus unacceptable for Roman Catholics, as is the "morning-after pill," since both cause a very early abortion of an already fertilized ovum.

An advantage of the IUD is that as long as it is in place, it needs no further attention. When the couple wants a child, the woman can simply have it removed. It is a highly effective birth control device.

The diaphragm and spermicidal jelly

The diaphragm has a large ring-shaped rim, with a thin, loose, air-tight sheet of rubber or plastic across it. It must be carefully fitted by a physician and refitted after every pregnancy. The woman spreads a coat of spermicidal jelly in it and inserts it into the vagina before intercourse so that it fully covers the entrance to the womb. The sperm-killing jelly helps destroy any live sperm that try to swim around the edges of the diaphragm.

This method is also highly effective and safe, though one couple I know used it faithfully and still had three of their five babies unplanned. It has to be inserted each time before intercourse. If it is properly inserted, neither party is aware of its presence during coitus. It must be left in place for at least six to eight hours after intercourse. After each use it must be washed and prepared for a future use.

The condom—only if tested

Of the four recommended methods, the condom or "rubber" is the only one that is used by the male, that is available with no doctor's prescription, and that provides some protection against venereal disease. It is therefore the method most often used by sexually active young, unmarried couples.

The condom is a supposedly air-tight covering that is rolled over the erect penis. It prevents sperm from reaching the vagina.

Condoms can be highly effective, but there is one catch. They must first be carefully tested for leaks. If not, they are only about 45% dependable, since they often contain small holes. Sperm are so tiny that they can escape through the smallest of holes. Since most young users do not bother to test them, they are not reliable.

A condom may be tested in two ways. It can be filled full of water and examined for leaks, or it can be inflated like a balloon and placed under water. If air bubbles appear anywhere, throw it away.

Unsafe at any speed

No other current methods of contraception are considered effective enough to count on. Withdrawal of the penis before ejaculation is unsafe for two reasons. First, there may be live sperm in the preseminal lubricant-like fluid that emerges from the penis during sexual excitement. Second, since the male must pull away at precisely the time when he least wants to do so, he may wait too long and eject sperm into the vagina.

The douche, or washing out the vagina, is of little value. It takes only seconds for some sperm to get

115

through the cervix. A douche will likely be much too late to be effective.

The so-called safe period is highly unsafe—in spite of the recent claims of improvements. The theory is that there is a period of time just before and just after menstruation when the female cannot conceive. But the theory limps on a lot of legs. It is often hard to pinpoint the time of ovulation. Some emotional upset or strain may alter a woman's schedule. Sperm can live much longer in a favorable environment than once thought. The couple must abstain for long periods of time—perhaps at the very times when they least want to do so. For many women ovulation is not regular. All in all, the safe period just is not safe. Other methods must be used if conception is to be dependably avoided.

Foams are not reliable of themselves, though they may add a margin of safety when used with one of the "favored four" methods.

Lack of sexual excitement in the woman is no help; she may be cold and unresponsive and still conceive. It happens all the time in rape cases.

The coital position used gives no protection either. As long as sperm gets into the vagina, the risk is great. Having sex in a sitting or standing position will not help at all.

In sum, no contraceptive is adequate except one of the favored four noted above. And even those are not 100% effective. The only sure way to avoid pregnancy is not to have intercourse at all.

Don't get the wrong idea

Just because I've outlined the best available ways to avert pregnancy doesn't mean that I condone their use by the unmarried couple. Don't think to yourself: "Whee! Prof. Short says it's OK to diddle—just as long as you play it safe!" Prof. Short takes quite the opposite view. In light of all the facts, I don't think it makes any sense at all to have full sex before you marry. The evidence is clear and overriding.

Now let's return to the remaining key clues to distinguish real love from infatuation and sexual attraction.

13 | How do you see each other?

There are two aspects of this clue. One has to do with the effect of your romance on your relationships with other people. The other deals with your ability to think straight about the object of your affections and your relationship.

Signs of infatuation

When infatuated, *you live in a one-person world.* Your attraction is like the earth's attraction to the sun —your whole universe revolves around that other person. Nothing else matters. No one else is important. You are all wrapped up in each other—perhaps literally!

When infatuated, you tend to neglect your family and pay little or no attention to your other friends. You turn a deaf ear to your teachers or your boss. You fail to do your homework. You lose interest in things that used to excite you.

Both of you tend to home in on that one relationship. It becomes not only the most important thing in your world, but the only thing that really matters to you. Your relationship tends to be exclusive. Your other friends feel left out, neglected, or ignored.

Since this "romantic love" (infatuation) is of such central concern to you, nothing must be allowed to stand in its way. You think you're justified in giving up anything in favor of this amazing event that has happened so unexpectedly.

One married woman with three children reports that within 48 hours after she first met a certain man at a lodge convention, she would have gone to bed with him. As it happened, they were both happy in their own marriages. Even so, she might have left her family and gone off with him, if he had pressed her to do so.

That couple was lucky. In a few weeks their ardor cooled and reason rescued them from their romantic emotions. Yet after many years they still have warm feelings toward each other. Many others are not so fortunate. They act rashly in the name of "love" and rue the day. But the damage is already done.

Signs of love

As with infatuation, in real love the beloved may well be the most important person in the world to you. But here's the big difference. In real love, you expand your world to include the beloved.

If you really love each other, you don't abandon or neglect your other relationships. Instead, you just *add this wonderful new relationship to all the others you have*. It becomes a plus, not a replacement.

You still maintain good ties with your family, your

friends, your teachers. You retain your interest in your studies—assuming that you had such an interest in the first place. Things that you liked to do before, you still like to do. Your world grows larger, not more narrow.

Is your beloved faultless?

Romantic infatuation is a vaccine that immunizes you against seeing anything wrong with the other person. You tend to put your beloved on a pedestal as a paragon of perfection. You live in a kind of romantic Disneyland.

No one can tell you anything wrong about the object of your affections. At best, you won't believe it. At worst, you may turn against the accuser in anger and rejection.

"You know, Bob," says a worried Dad, "I think that girl is a gossip. You should have heard what she said about her brother's wife."

"You don't understand her, Dad," counters Bob, dashing to the defense. "She's not a gossip. She just likes people!"

Or Mom may say, "Judy, I think your young man is a drunk. When I saw him last night in town, he could hardly stand up. If it hadn't been for the lamp post, he'd have fallen flat on his face in the gutter."

"Oh, no, Mom," she chirps. "He never gets drunk. He just gets to feeling good!" If Mom could buy that young man for his actual worth and sell him for what Judy thinks he's worth, Mom would be a millionaire.

If you're infatuated, you defend the other person against all critics. You just will not admit that he or she has any faults. This is idealization. You idealize not only each other, but also your situation. You two

120

may have gross problems and obstacles to cope with—different religions, hopes, values, family and cultural backgrounds. Danger signals by the dozen! Yet you are not concerned. You don't even feel the need to think about these enormous hazards before marriage. You think that somehow it all just has to come out OK. Your great "love" will see you through.

The tendency to idealize is very strong in our culture. Elsie King found that two-thirds of the women and more than half the men she studied had unrealistic views of the person they were about to wed.[1]

What makes us idealize so much? For one thing, we tend to be on our best behavior while courting. We show only our best side. Another reason is the "halo effect," or the tendency to judge the whole personality largely in terms of one or two highly admired qualities. One great trait or two can fool us into thinking that the whole person is great as well.

And sex gets into the act, too. One study showed that male subjects who were sexually aroused rated the pictures of the same girls to be much more attractive than did males who were not aroused. The greater his sexual need, the better the girl looked to the male.[2] *If infatuated, you'll tend to see what you want to see—*and need to see—in the other person, rather than what is really there.

If it's love, on the other hand, you admit their faults but love in spite of them. You will idealize the other person to some degree, even in real love. It is a matter of how much and what kind.

In infatuation, you tend to project what you want to see onto the other. You create the ideal, even if the elements of the ideal are not there. In love, you see the person's real merits and build on that. A mutual process is set in motion. Your love leads you to appreciate the best in the other. In turn, as the other person learns of your love, it brings out the best in her or him. You are frank to admit that the other is not perfect. But you see so much to be admired and respected that you can live with those faults.

Is love blind?

No, but infatuation is. Infatuation, like other extreme emotions such as anger, hate, and fear, distorts thinking. It is most deceptive. Infatuated persons prefer feeling to thinking. Only the passing of time will bring about gradual return to reality. When the ideal bubble bursts—and burst it will—pain and disillusionment sets in.

Again, it pays to be honest. Much of the pain and tragedy of romantic infatuation could be avoided if the couple would level with themselves and with each other. Instead, they hide their faults and mislead the other into thinking they are something they are not.

For this they pay an awful price. "Perhaps the most important reason for self-disclosure is that without it we cannot truly love. How can I love a person I don't know? How can the other person love me if he doesn't know me?" These questions posed by Sidney Jourard and Ardis Whitman are food for thought. Their answer? That honesty is a must.[3]

In this sense, they suggest that we behave like small children and "act our real selves." Perhaps this is what Jesus meant when he said one must become as a little child to enter the kingdom of God. It may also be the way to enter the kingdom of love.

Time is the infatuated person's best friend. It is both the great revealer and the great healer. When your heart has been broken, time will heal the hurt.

Time also is the best antidote for the deadly poison of idealization. "As interaction increases, knowledge converts the dream image into awareness of the real partner. Awareness punctures the dream bubble and brings the relationship down to earth." [4] Time can shield you from plunging into an unsound marriage on the strength of a mere infatuation. Love that is time tested is the real thing.

14 | How do others view you?

What do your friends and parents think about your relationship? We often hear some young person say: "Why should it matter to us if other people don't approve of our romance? After all, we're marrying each other, not each other's families and friends."

That is in part true, but in a very real sense you *do* marry your mate's family and friends. You marry all that he or she identifies with and cares about. That includes friends and family.

Signs of infatuation

If you are infatuated, chances are that *your parents and most of your friends do not approve* of your relationship. Your beloved's friends likely don't think much of you, and your friends aren't very fond of him or her, either. They may not come right out and say it to your face, but they wish you'd "hurry up and come to your senses."

In infatuation, each of you will also dislike the other's friends. He may think—if not say—that he can hardly stand to be around "those idiots she calls her friends." And she may wonder what possible good he sees in "that bunch of baboons" he runs around with.

All of this can be a warning signal. You will do well to think carefully before you marry.

Signs of love

If it's love, *most or all friends and parents approve.* You like each other's friends and feel comfortable with them, because you have a good deal in common. In rare cases a "best friend" may feel jealous, hence resentful of the time you two love birds spend together. But for the most part, there is mutual acceptance and friendliness.

Why do friends tend to approve when it's real love and not approve if it's infatuation? If you've taken geometry you may recall one of the main postulates: "Things equal to the same thing are equal to each other." That applies to this clue.

Over the years, both you and your beloved have developed a circle of friends of the same sex. Now ask yourself: What brings friends of the same sex together? If you are heterosexual you choose same-sex friends not on the basis of sexual attraction, but because of their personalities and because you have lots of interests in common. You like to talk about and do many of the same things.

In infatuation, you have been drawn to each other by physical attraction. This is completely different from what attracted you to your same-sex friends. Therefore, since the two of you have few interests in common, few if any of your friends approve of your choice.

On the other hand, if you really love each other, your relationship is also based on the many interests you share. You are friends as well as lovers. Now remember, things equal to the same thing are equal to each other. Since you like in each other the same kinds of things you like in your friends of the same sex, then all of you have a great deal in common. You all have lots to talk about, many of the same interests, a great many similar ideas. Thus you are all far more likely to get along well together. So most or all of your friends will approve of your relationship.

Judson T. and Mary Landis have summarized this idea.

> Two who love each other must be friends in the same sense that any two people of the same sex are friends. This means they enjoy each other's company because of genuine congeniality, aside from sexual interest; they want to confide in each other, to talk things over, and to share amusement, ideas, disappointment or grief. They tend to see life through each other's eyes. They are at ease and comfortable with each other, as good friends always are.[1]

So if few or none of your friends approve of your boy or girl friend, beware. Your "love" interest is probably based on physical attraction and sex. But if many friends approve, that suggests that you have much mutuality, many things in common. These factors are basic elements in a real love relationship. It follows, then, if most of your friends approve, you are more likely in love.

Kelly suggests several thoughtful questions to ask

yourself. "Can you be yourself naturally with the person you love? Does he or she bring out the best in you, or the worst? Are you genuinely proud of [this person]? Do you enjoy being with him [or her] in the company of your family and friends?" [2]

To these queries we would add one more. Are the same qualities present in your beloved that you like in your same-sex friends? If they are not present, proceed with caution. It may be just infatuation, not love.

Do parents approve?

Whether your parents approve of your romance is another key part of this clue. When parents do not approve of a marriage, the failure rates are very high.

Most parents love their children. If you are a teenager, you may find that hard to believe. They may not let you have movie money or the car keys as often as you'd like. You may not get to stay out as late as you want. Still, mature parents want to see their children happy, both now and in the future. Your parents probably want you to have all the good things that life can bring. That includes a happy marriage.

So if your parents think you're about to make a big mistake, they are likely to oppose it. They don't want you to get hurt, to be robbed of future joy. If they're convinced you're making a poor choice, they just may be right. Since they don't have stars in their eyes like you do, they may be able to see the situation more clearly than you can. If so, then they are being your friends, not your enemies, by showing their concern or by not approving of the relationship.

There is one exception to this. A minority of parents may be emotionally immature, not willing or able to release sons or daughters to live their own lives. No girl is ever quite good enough for darling Junior. Or if sister brought home the angel Gabriel himself, Dad would find fault with him. In such cases, if the young person is ever to marry he or she must do so against the parent's wishes.

But if your parents object, be very sure it is they who are immature and not yourself. You may just be looking for an excuse to believe that they are wrong and you are right. You may be kidding yourself again.

It's usually a mistake for parents to "lay down the law" and forbid their children to see the person they object to. That will probably just drive the couple into each other's arms. They may resolve to show them what's what, so they'll slip out and meet anyway. This is known as the Romeo-and-Juliet effect, since these famed lovers had families who staunchly opposed their courtship. Studies have shown that parental opposition may actually cause a couple to fall deeper into "romantic love" or infatuation.[3] In time, this effect usually wears off, however, so don't marry foolishly just to spite your parents. You'd be cutting off your nose to spite your face.

Scientific support

There is strong evidence that peer and parental approval tend to indicate love. Harvey J. Locke compared complaints registered by happily married persons with those of divorced individuals. Divorced persons were almost four times as likely to complain that they and their spouses had no mutual friends. That is, they seemed to have little in common with the other's friends. Locke also found that happily married couples were far less likely to have problems with each other's parents. Divorced men were three times as likely to list "interference of in-laws" as a major complaint.[4] This bears out the view that real loves are more likely to gain the approval of parents.

So be alert to note what others think of your choice. When most friends and parents object, take special care. They are trying to tell you something you should know.

But if most or all of them approve, that is a good sign. Take heart. And the more there are who approve, the more likely it is that you've found real love.

15 | What does distance do?

Many things can separate a young couple. Families move away, young people go off to school or work or military service. If you're apart, you may feel anxious as well as sad. "What if one of us finds someone else?" you may worry.

Will your interest in each other pull through the strain, or will it die out? These concerns are not without cause. Studies show that engaged couples are more likely to break up if they're separated.

Signs of infatuation

If it is infatuation, absence makes the heart grow fonder—of somebody else. In infatuation Sue and Sam have been interested mainly in each other's physical equipment. That interest is hard to sustain when they're separated by a thousand miles. Since only a few things attract them to each other, the roots of the relationship are thin. It won't last long unless it gets nourished by a lot of face-to-face contact.

After the infatuated couple is apart for a few days or weeks, they begin to lose interest. It's not much of a thrill to kiss a photograph goodnight. After a while the physical equipment of some more available persons begins to look good to them. So if it is infatuation, *it will die with distance.* It cannot survive the added strain of separation.

Signs of love

Love survives separation. It may even grow. Absence does indeed make the heart grow fonder. Why? Because love is rooted in attraction to the other's total personality, not just physical appeal. When you are in love, a great many of the tendrils of your personalities tend to grow together, to unite you into loving oneness. When you have to be apart, you are not your whole self. When the other person is not there, *you* are not all there. Something vital is missing, and you long to be reunited. You realize how much your relationship means to you.

So if a separation comes, don't worry about it. If you do find that it's infatuation and hence doesn't survive, be grateful—it's a good thing you found out before it was too late. On the other hand, if you survive the separation, it may be real love.

16 | How do quarrels affect the romance?

Even a couple united by love will quarrel once in a while. Any time two people seek to merge the many facets of their personalities, there will be rough edges to iron out.

So be prepared for some friction even if you're in love. You will disagree on a few things. Some aspects of your lives won't fit together well, at least not right away. There will be many adjustments to make, and sparks may fly at times until you get things worked out between you.

Sometimes a couple will tell me, "We've been married 20 years and never had a quarrel." Well, bless their angelic little hearts! When I hear that, I suspect that one of three things is true.

First, they may be lying through their teeth. They've quarreled and they know it. They just won't admit it.

Second, they quite honestly may have forgotten. Over the years a couple may well discover more creative and constructive ways to settle disputes. They may learn to tether tongues and fetter feelings. They don't argue, they discuss. They learn the art of give and take. So since it may have been many years since they last quarreled, they may have forgotten that they ever did.

Third, if a couple have in fact been married 20 years and never had a quarrel, at least one of them is probably a "Milquetoast"—a doormat who does not stand up for his or her own personal rights. That's not a marriage, that's enslavement.

So the important thing is not whether you quarrel, but the way you quarrel. Ask yourself three questions. 1. How severe are your quarrels? 2. How often do they occur? 3. What is the final effect of quarrels on your relationship? The answers are good indications of the nature of your romance.

Signs of infatuation

In infatuation, *quarrels will kill the relationship, and they tend to become more frequent and more severe.* Since your main attraction is physical and the number of interests you hold in common are few, the few things you do have in common soon prove too weak to give lasting support. The fabric of your romance starts to wear thin. You begin to lose interest. You find yourselves disagreeing on more and more things, so more and more often you quarrel. The words get more harsh and full of mean barbs. You hurt each other more and more deeply—and you may do it on purpose.

After each quarrel, you kiss and make up. (That part is oh, so wonderful, be it love or infatuation.) But your renewed closeness does not last. The bonds between you continue to go to pieces. Finally, the sour times overshadow the sweet. One or both of you decide that it's not worth the struggle. Hard as it is to do so, you break it off. You may go back together a time or two, but there are no bonds of love. In time, you break for good and go your separate ways—be it before or after marriage.

Signs of love

If it is love, the opposite is true. *Love lives through quarrels, and quarrels become less frequent and less severe.* A loving couple has a broader base of things in common. Their relationship can absorb a good deal of strain because it has a firmer foundation.

In love you feel more a part of each other, so you have more of a stake in working things out. You see a future together and seek to claim it. You try harder to find good substitutes for conflict. You learn to communicate in more creative ways.

For instance, you can learn to discuss frankly without arguing. Nobody wins an argument; it just confirms both of you more solidly in your own views. One couple makes it a practice never to reply in anger, no matter how great the urge to do so. "Just as it takes two to tango, it takes two to tangle," the girl explained. "When one of us gets angry, the other just shuts up until the dust settles. It works, too."

"I'm sorry" may well be the hardest words you'll ever say. But atonements bring at-homeness. It is only common courtesy to show others that we regret a past mistake. Such an admission will likely call forth warm acceptance and response in kind from the other person. Does love really mean never having to say you're sorry? On the contrary, we should never take the forgiveness of another for granted, no matter how deep

134

the love bond between us. Maybe our loved one does not demand that we say it, but it will be much appreciated if we do.

So quarrels, while common, are not crucial. There are other ways to settle disputes, and loving couples need to find them.

Constructive quarreling

Some writers hold that conflict is not only normal, but necessary. They even offer rules on how to fight. I doubt this is the best approach for the average couple.

However, conflict between two people who love each other can serve a useful purpose. Quarrels can be constructive. Just as an electrical fuse serves to keep a sudden burst of strong current from blowing out the whole power system, an occasional quarrel will cause brief grief, but it may avert even greater marital damage. It may be better to blow off some steam and spoil an evening than to blow the whole relationship.

Jim and Jill have been married for some months. Each of them has found a few frustrating faults in the other. Jim hides behind his paper at breakfast when she'd like to talk, and Jill talks with her mother a lot by phone. They find these things somewhat irritating, but say nothing. After all, they love each other and do not wish to offend.

Then one day Jim comes home after a bad day at the office. (You know the old story. Dad gets chewed out by his boss, he comes home and fusses at Mom, Mom yells at Junior, and Junior goes out and kicks the dog.) Jill is on the phone with you know who—and the soup is starting to scorch.

Jim explodes. "Can't you stop talking to that woman

long enough to get a meal?" Jill's jaw drops. Hurt and shocked, she bangs down the receiver.

"Well, if you'd come out from behind your paper once in a while, I wouldn't need to talk to Mom so much," she shoots back. Then the argument really heats up.

Before long they calm down and feel sorrow and shame. They embrace. Each one tries to take full blame for the outburst. Soon all is well again.

All may be well, but all is not the same. What has happened that may be a plus for their future together? For one thing, they leveled with each other. They brought their gripes out in the open instead of bottling them up.

Resentment and tensions may build up and fester into more serious problems. "Unless you say 'ouch,' your partners cannot know that they are stepping on your toes." [1] Now that Jim and Jill have alerted each other to things that bother them, they are likely to avoid doing those same things in the future.

Quarrels can be dangerous

While they may do some good, quarrels can also do a lot of harm. Some studies show that quarrels may act more as a hair trigger than a safety valve. Murray Strauss found that as an argument heats up, so does the probability that the couple will resort to body blows.[2] If she throws a harsh remark at him, she's more likely to follow it up with the frying pan. This would scarcely qualify as a constructive quarrel.

Perhaps the key to constructive conflict is mutual caring and respect. A principle of child rearing could apply here. If a child ever has to be spanked, it should be done out of love, never out of anger or spite. The punishment should hurt the parent as much as the child—though maybe not in the same place!

So it should be with marital quarrels. When the couple talks straight with each other, there should never be any doubt about an underlying bond of love. Each should be quite sure that the other deeply cares and is supportive, not destructive. The quarrel should not leave the partners hostile, hurt, angry, or bitter. The motive is to make the relationship better, not to tear down or destroy it—and each other.

CLUE ELEVEN

17 | How do you feel about and refer to your relationship?

This is a very subtle clue. You will have to catch yourself off guard to apply it. But if you succeed, it will tell you how you feel about the other person in your subconscious or inner mind. It will help you unmask any play-acting you may unwittingly be doing in relation to each other. That way you can avoid fooling yourself—and the other person, too.

Inner feelings are revealing

Your deep inner feelings can be detected by observing closely the way you refer to yourself, to your beloved, and to your relationship. If you have trouble applying this test to yourself, alert a good friend to do it for you.

Suppose that you have a sister who thinks she's found her Mr. Wonderful. You're still up when she comes in from their date. She has a stardust look in her eyes.

138

"How was your date?" you ask.

"Oh," she sighs, "just great. He's the most wonderful guy in the whole world."

Now's your chance. Play it cool and draw her out. "Oh?" you say innocently. "Tell me all about it." Then note with great care the words she uses to refer to herself and her young man. She may not tell you *all* about her date, but see if you can learn whether she's really in love from what she says.

"Well," your unsuspecting sister says, "he came to pick me up at a quarter past eight. He was supposed to come at eight, but he was late as usual. I didn't want him to think I was just waiting around for him, so I pretended I wasn't ready yet. I didn't go down for a full 10 minutes.

"Out at his car, do you know what? He opened the door for me! 'Well,' I said, 'chivalry isn't dead!'"

" 'Oh, yes it is,' he said. 'I just forgot.' I nearly died laughing. He's so clever.

"Well, I really liked that movie. It's just the kind I like best. Lot's of creepy, crawly spiders and snakes.

" 'Are you afraid?' he whispered.

"I said, 'Oh, not when I'm with you, John.' And he squeezed me so hard I had to cough!

"After the movie I said I was hungry, so he took me to the drive-in. He had a hot dog with soya sauce and I had a hamburger with Limburger cheese . . ."

End of story. Now what are you hearing—besides an awful menu? How was she referring to him, to herself, and to her date? What were the key words she used?

Signs of infatuation

Time and again she used the words *I*, *me*, *my*, and *he*, *him*, *his*. She did not once use words like *we*, *us*, or *our*. She was unwittingly revealing her true feelings. By the use of these terms she has betrayed that she is still keeping her own identity carefully separate from his. It was "I did this" and "he said that" and "this happened to me (or to him)."

That tells us that she has not yet come to think of herself as part of a couple. She has not yet invested her self in the relationship. She's still clinging to her own selfish identity. That points to infatuation.

Signs of love

Two persons who have real love, on the other hand, come to feel that they are no longer separate, but have in great measure become one. Since they see themselves as a unit, they tend to use *we* and *us* and *our* when they refer to what happens to them. It seems only natural and right to do so.

Reik cites an example from the Orient to illustrate this merging of two persons into a kind of oneness.

> Kuan Tao-Sheng, the wife of the great Chinese painter Chao Mang-Fu, felt that her husband had withdrawn his affection from her and bestowed it upon a mistress. She wrote this poem:
>
> > Take a lump of clay,
> > Wet it, pat it,
> > Make a statue of you
> > And a statue of me.
> > Then shatter them, clatter them,
> > Add some water,
> > And break them and mold them
> > Into a statue of you
> > And a statue of me.
> > Then in mine, there are bits of you
> > And in you there are bits of me.
> > Nothing ever shall keep us apart.[1]

Kuan Tao-Sheng won again the affection of her husband.

The couple truly in love are no longer two, but one, or rather two *in* one. "It is not implied that the two personalities disappear in this union," J.L. Hirning points out. "They are simply so much alike in motivation, attitudes, values, interests and viewpoints that the differences between them are reduced to a minimum. There results a strong feeling of oneness; each person feels fully accepted, protected, and secure." They are still unique, separate persons, but they merge themselves into a pattern of common bonds. In this sense they have become "unselfed." [2]

Love is a paradox

A paradox is something that sounds like a lie—a contradiction—but is actually a great truth. Love is a paradox. In love, the couple give up much of their separate selves, yet by doing so each becomes even more fulfilled as a self. Individuality is not stifled by love; it is enriched. As they become a "we," each is at once a more fulfilled "I." They get double enjoyment out of everything they do. In the first place, each of them enjoys things as individuals just as they did before they were in love. But in addition, they have the added joy of sharing those things with the loved one.

The other side of the coin is that you may not want to do or enjoy things by yourself, unless the beloved is able to share them. "I don't want to go unless you can go, too, dear," is a common response of lovers. Real love is happiest when "we" do things together, not separately. Your own joy is incomplete unless you can share it with your love, either at the time or later.

18 | Are you selfish or selfless?

Clues 12 and 13 may well be the two most important in the list. They have to do with whether a couple are self-centered or other-centered. They deal with the basic, core attitude that each person displays toward the other. Such elements will be crucial to the success or failure of any marriage.

Signs of infatuation

Carl really likes to date Kate, who's the school's "super doll." Not that he likes her all that much. She is pretty and popular, but she's also spoiled and demanding. Still, he likes to date her because, since she's the "queen" of the school, dating her makes him "king." He's the envy of all the fellows when they see him out with her. So he dates her, not for herself, but for the boost it gives to his ego.

If you are infatuated, *your ego response to the other*

person is mainly selfish and restrictive. Your prime interest in the relationship is what it does for *you.*

Infatuated persons say, "I really feel important when I'm with him" or "She really turns me on." The stress is selfish. They don't think about whether the other person's desires or needs are being filled. The key concern is that the person's own needs are served.

Other remarks that suggest selfishness are:

"I'm happier when I'm with him than I am with any other boy."

"If you loved me, you'd let me have sex with you."

"I'm not sure you could make me happy for the rest of my life."

"I know you love to dance (watch football), but I don't—so I don't see why we should go to the prom (game)."

Maybe you know someone who keeps a guy "on the string." She doesn't care much for him, but his devotion to her builds up her self-image.

Then there's the guy who keeps wanting to make his partner over to suit himself. He is not content that she be herself. He wants to change her into the person he wants or needs her to be. These are both examples of selfish infatuation.

It's not wrong for you to have your personal needs filled. Every person needs that. But when your overriding interest is your own selfish wants and needs, when you have little or no concern for the wants and needs of your partner—then that's not love, it's infatuation.

Selfish sex

Some guys date girls just for the thrill of necking or petting. In extreme cases, according to Reik, sex is

143

utterly selfish, using the object only to get satisfaction. If a man's interest in a woman is just sex, then when he is through having sex with her, he is through with her, period—until he gets the urge to have sex again.

One instance of this was observed in the American South some years ago. A white man was having intercourse with a black woman. Just as it was over, she reached up and kissed him—and he slapped her! His interest in her was solely for sex. He did not want her to feel or express any affection, since he had none for her. Her "place" was to submit, not respond.

By contrast, Reik thinks that "in no case can love be only selfish, or as selfish as sex. . . . It is always concerned with the welfare or happiness of the other person, regrets the other's absence [even right after sex], wants to be together with the object, feels lonely without it." [1]

Signs of love

If it is love, *your ego response tends to be unselfish and outgoing.* You care as much about what's good for the other as for yourself. You want her or him to get as much out of the relationship as you get. Love "is a state in which each one of two people realizes that his happiness can be attained only when the other also is happy. As a consequence, each one lives not only for himself but for the other, sometimes even more for the other than for himself." [2]

If you're in love, you will share thoughts, feelings, attitudes, plans, hopes, interests, even intimate things you would share with few if any others. And the more you share, the more committed to each other you will become. If you are in love, you will also want to keep these shared secrets pretty private—even sacred. You will shy away from obvious necking and petting in public. It is no accident that those who display a lot of affection in public also tend to get low scores on emotional maturity tests.

Commitment—a law of life

Not only is the unselfish commitment of one's self essential to a happy marriage, it is important to gaining fullness of life in any area. One of the basic secrets of life is that a higher fulfillment of self comes as a result of committing one's self to something higher and greater than the self. Such a commitment helps us to rise above mere concern with our own selfish ego. It opens whole new horizons of value and meaning for our lives. The person least concerned about self is the person who becomes most fulfilled. This paradox was set forth by Jesus of Nazareth: "Whoever tries to save his life will lose it; whoever loses his life will save it." [3]

If you love a spouse or a family not for themselves, but because they are *your* spouse and *your* children, then that is selfish—another kind of self-love. This, like any other type of self-love, serves to keep you from finding fulfillment. So if you are to be fully mature, your circle of concern needs to reach not just beyond the self, but beyond your own family and local community as well.

To love another means that you wish to protect him or her from all harm. Since some threats to life are global—pollution, nuclear war, population growth—so must your concern be worldwide. We need to be citizens of the world. [4] As George Wald once said, our concern must be with not only *what kind* of a future this generation will have, but *whether* they have a future at all.

145

19 | What is your overall attitude?

Closely related to your ego response is your general attitude toward your partner. Are you concerned solely with what you get out of the relationship? Or do you find yourself wanting to make sure the other person is happy, and that his or her needs are also being met?

Signs of infatuation

If you are infatuated, your overall attitude is one of *taking from the relationship*. You will find that your main concern is what you are getting out of it, plus what you hope to get in the future. The other person is seen as a means to gratify your own personal needs and wants, to attain your own goals and satisfactions.

You like the person *not* for what he or she is as a person, but for what that person does for you. You use the person as a stepping-stone to get things you want. Your partner helps you get attention, go places you like, satisfy your sex urge, climb the social ladder, get out of a bad home life, or a host of other private ends. In short, you exploit the other. If your main concern is to "look out for Number 1"—namely yourself—then look out. You are infatuated.

Such an attitude will not help you build a long, happy relationship. If you are willing to use the person for your own advantage before you marry, you will no doubt do so afterward as well. You will marry not for love, but for self-centered reasons such as greed or lust, position or prestige, a life of ease or security. These are scarcely the elements of real love. They grow instead out of selfishness and pride, which are in turn rooted in your ego response to the other person.

Signs of love

If you have found real love, you more and more want to give to, not take from, the other person and the relationship. *You want to share, give of your self to your beloved.* You are intent on doing all you can to bring happiness to the other just as long as it does not spoil chances for his or her future fulfillment, or threaten your future together.

In years past it was the custom for the man to propose to his beloved on bended knee. "I want to spend my life making you happy," he would say. If he really meant that, if he was honestly longing to give of himself to bring fulfillment to his sweetheart, he was truly in love.

When you are in love, you want your beloved to be as happy as you are. Your concern for that person and his or her welfare is on a par with concern for yourself. The beloved has come to be a part of you. You cannot be truly happy unless that person is happy, too.

If you haven't yet reached that stage, then you probably do not love.

When you do reach this level of love, it may inspire a similar love in your beloved. Theodor Reik tells of the courtship of Moses Mendelssohn, the philosopher with a deformed body. Born small of stature and a hunchback, he fell in love with the daughter of a rich nobleman. She was so repelled by his looks that he had no chance to reveal to her his true self.

One day as he was leaving the city, he asked to bid her farewell.

> He found her busy with some needlework. She avoided looking at him during their conversation. Cleverly he led her around to the subject which was in his mind. She asked him whether he too believed that marriages are made in Heaven. "Certainly," he replied: "and something quite unusual happened to me. As you know, they call out in Heaven at the birth of a child, 'This one and that one will get this and that girl for a wife.' When I was born, my future wife was also thus announced, but it was added: 'She will, alas, have a terrible hump.' I shouted: 'Oh, God, Lord, a girl who is humpbacked will very easily become bitter and hard. A girl should be beautiful. Good Lord, give the hump to me and let her be handsome and well formed.'" The girl, deeply moved, stretched out her hand for Mendelssohn's. She became his faithful and loving wife.[1]

His tale of self-giving love, which conveyed the point that his own love was of like kind, helped her to look beyond his body and see his real self. She could tell that he knew what true love is all about. As Robert Blood says:

> It involves concern for the partner, interest in his welfare, and effort to meet his needs. Caring is

> intensely personal. The ministry of care is carried
> on joyously. He who truly cares never considers
> himself a martyr or deserving of special praise.[2]

Love is not used up in the giving. The more of it you give away, the more of it you have. Like a mountain spring, the supply seems endless.

Along with the receiver of love, the giver of love gets joyous rewards. The one who gives feels needed and useful. Some people say that all love is selfish. Since the one who loves and gives of self will in return get the reward of feeling useful, they claim, then that is also selfish. They see every human relationship as a selfish exchange, a give and take in the human marketplace. There is some truth in that view. Each of us does have needs, and we do seek to fill them.

But to assume that all love is selfish is to miss the main point of that paradox Jesus described. It is to confuse the intent of an act with the results of that act. "Whoever tries to save his life will lose it." If you set out to save your life, that's a selfish *intent*. The *result* is that you lose out on life. You miss the joy of giving, of being useful, of feeling needed.

"Whoever loses his life will save it." The intent here is to lose or forego selfish self-fulfillment. And if you do that, what is the result? You actually get more of life. Why? Because you not only share the joys of the other person, but you also get lots of extra unsought joys as well—the joys of being useful and feeling needed.

Putting our finger on a rule of thumb

Teenagers sometimes ask me, "Can't you give us one simple rule we can use to tell whether it's love?"

In one sense, no one rule can be enough. Each of

the 14 clues is important, each should be fully considered. But if I were forced to come up with just one key clue to help you determine whether you truly love, here's what it would be. It will separate the men from the boys and the women from the girls pretty fast.

If you love someone so much that you want that person to be happy, even if you are not the one to make him or her happy, then you really love that person. That is, if you love someone so much that you want that person to be happy, even if you can't be the one who *shares* that happiness, then your love is indeed real.

It is natural that, if you love a person, you long to be near, to share all life with that person. But if you love him or her enough, you'll want that person to be happy, whether or not you get to share it.

If you are old enough and mature enough to marry, and if you find someone who loves you like that—and you feel the same way in return—think a long, long time before you let him or her get away. There aren't many loves like that around. If you find one, hang on to it if you can.

In most cases, of course, such love need not be denied. The couple will spend their lives together, devoted to the joy of making each other happy.

But what if you come to feel that you are not good for your beloved? Is your love so deep, is your desire for that person's happiness so great, that you are willing to give him or her up if you think it is best? That is the acid test of love.

But be sure you have read the signs right before you give up such a love. One young woman made a bad mistake.

Pam dearly loved a young man who was going into

150

the ministry. But she had been divorced—and she knew that his church strongly opposed divorce. She concluded that if she were to marry him, it would spoil his life work. So she swallowed her own deep desire to marry him and gave him no encouragement when he tried to court her. He therefore thought she didn't love him, so they drifted apart.

His church later became much less rigid on the matter of divorce, and he eventually married a divorced woman. Pam remarried, but after many years she still loved that young minister. She had loved him enough to give him up, only to find that she had misread his needs and her ability to fill them. It is a bitter memory for them both. So proceed with care if you're considering giving up a true love.

CLUE FOURTEEN

20 | Are you jealous?

Jealousy may be a cultural universal. It pops up in all kinds of patterns and places. A new dad resents mom's time with the baby. Junior resents the second child. Siblings become rivals. Spouses and sweethearts grow jealous if their beloveds show the slightest sign of fondness toward a rival—real or imagined.

Anthropologists find jealousy near and far. No society seems to be without it, even those in which more than one spouse is the accepted rule, and those where adultery is fully permitted.[1]

Even so-called liberals with "open" marriages or live-in arrangements do not escape the green-eyed monster.[2] "True, there may very well be people who are secure enough within themselves not to be threatened by their spouse's openly having a sex relationship with another person," observes James McCary. "But, as Gracie Allen used to say, 'There are a lot of people like that, but not many.'"[3]

Even Nena O'Neill, formerly an ardent advocate of sexually open marriages, has changed her mind. She's found that open marriage has not worked for couples who have tried it, due to jealousy. She now advocates "one sexual partner for the rest of your life." [4] So you too may well feel jealous, whether you're in love or infatuated.

Why are we jealous?

Some authorities say jealousy is a sign that we are insecure and unsure of ourselves; we have a "low self-image." [5] Others believe the roots of jealousy go back to childhood dependency when we tried to lay exclusive claim to our mother's love and care. Some think that groups of two persons lend themselves to a jealous desire to hold on to each other. "The sensitive union of two is always irritated by the spectator," even if the persons are mature and secure.[6]

Whatever its cause, the green-eyed monster provides us with the last clue to unlock the puzzle of love and infatuation. This clue is saved for last, not because jealousy is so important in itself. It is not. But its function can best be understood in the light of the two clues that precede it—ego response and overall attitude.

Signs of infatuation

Some people think jealousy is a true measure of love. They assume that the more jealous you are, the more you love your sweetheart. A young woman once said, "Oh, Prof, he must love me so very much. If I even look at another boy, he blows his stack. He's so jealous he gets purplish green with rage." Is that real love? It clearly is not.

It is in infatuation, not love, that *jealousy is frequent*

153

and severe. When you're jealous you want to fence the other person in, to keep him or her wholly to yourself. You are, in short, being selfish and possessive. Your concern is with what *you* want, not with what the other person wants. You're afraid that he or she might enjoy—or give some attention to—someone other than yourself.

Such a response is selfish. Your attitude is one of *taking* from your relationship. You are not willing to release the other person to do freely what he or she finds enjoyable. In effect, you are saying: "I want you to be happy, but only if you do what makes *me* happy. My happiness comes first, not yours." That is a sign of infatuation, not love.

Since marriages based on infatuation are much more likely to fail, it comes as no surprise that jealousy is strongly associated with divorce. More than three times as many divorced than happily married persons report mate jealousy.[7]

So jealousy is not a good sign—it is a danger signal. It does not cement a love relationship, it breaks it apart. The more jealousy there is, the more likely it is that you're infatuated.

Signs of love

If it is love, *jealousy is less frequent and less severe.* Not that you will never feel jealous. None of us ever gets to be fully selfless. But the more you love the other person, the more you are able to release her or him. "Release is an expression of trust, respect, and acceptance."[8] To the extent that your love is not selfish, you can be free of jealousy.

If she likes to talk to another boy once in a while, he will not restrain her freedom. He wants her to be happy, even though he might prefer that she talk with him all the time. She will not mind if he on occasion likes to dance with some other girl. Love does not restrict, it releases. It does not imprison, it liberates.

That's why it's so important that love be mutual. If you love, you trust. That means you need someone worthy of that trust. That way you can free each other to be your true selves, in full confidence that your trust will not be betrayed.

Slaying the green-eyed monster

But isn't it all right to try to make your beloved jealous once in a while, just so he or she will pay more attention to you? Not if you love him or her. That kind of pressure tactic is selfish. Love never tries to hurt the beloved.

In one sense, if members of the opposite sex are attracted to your beloved, it is a compliment to you. After all, who wants to admit to choosing someone so dull and unattractive that no other person would find him or her interesting? That your beloved is worthy of the notice of others is something to be proud of, not a cause for misery and fear.

As your love grows, so does your trust and confidence. More and more you learn to avoid the things that displease each other. As a result, jealousy comes to be less frequent and less severe. At length it may all but disappear.

21 | Putting it all together

We can now put all 14 clues together and construct a useful tool to describe the kind of love that will support a marriage.

Remember that no one clue alone tells you enough to judge the nature of a relationship. Instead, see how your romance stacks up with regard to the entire 14.

You must be utterly honest with yourself to get a sound, accurate reading. If you cheat, you only cheat yourself. But if you use the clues with care and good judgment, they will help you make the right choice.

The love/infatuation chart

The chart on pages 158–59 can help you make an accurate tally of how your romance scores on the love/infatuation continuum. After reading the 14 clues, you probably have a general impression of whether you're really in love. But to make such a great decision, you need a more accurate assessment.

Examine each clue with studied care. Give it a good deal of thought. Take all the time you need.

You want to find out not only whether a clue indicates you're in love, but also the degree to which it indicates that. You want to detect shades of difference in each of your ratings. So simply rate each clue on a scale of zero to 10. Zero stands for complete infatuation, 10 for pure love.

0	1	2	3	4	5	6	7	8	9	10
Infatuation					About even					Love

Give each clue careful thought to see how it applies in your case. Think of as many aspects of the clue as you can, and the ways they affect you and your partner. Then choose the number on the scale which, by your soundest judgment, seems the most accurate description of your situation.

Take, for example, Clue 8: Do friends and parents approve? Suppose that you and your partner each have three close friends, and your parents are all living. If all but two of these ten friends and parents approve, your score would be 8. If only your mother and two of your sweetheart's friends approve, you score 3. If none approves, you get a goose egg!

Unless you're rating a past romance, only 13 of the clues will apply. You can't tell how it will end if it hasn't ended yet, so Clue 6 cannot be rated. This means that a perfect love score for a current romance is 130 points—10 points each for 13 clues.

When you have rated your romance on all of the clues, add up all the numbers to get your total score.

What your scores mean

The higher your score is, of course the more likely it is that you have real love. If you score 90 or above,

14 key clues to distinguish infatuation and love

CHARACTERISTICS

CLUES Questions to ask	If it's romantic infatuation	If it's real love
The nature of the attraction		
1. What is your main interest? What attracts you most?	Person's "physical equipment"; the body; what responds to the five senses.	The total personality; whole person; what's *in* the body.
2. How many things attract you?	Few—though some may be strong.	Many or most.
The course of the romance		
3. How did the romance start?	Fast (hours or days).	Slowly (months or years).
4. How consistent is your level of interest?	Interest varies, comes and goes; many peaks and valleys; not consistent or predictable.	Evens out; gets to be dependable, consistent; can predict it.
5. What effect does the romance have on your personality?	Disorganizing, destructive; you act strangely, are not "yourself."	Organizing, constructive; you're a better person.
6. How does it end?	Fast—*unless* there's been mutually satisfying sex.	Slowly; takes long time; you may never be quite the same.
Two views of you two		
7. How do you view each other?	You live in a one-person world. You see the other as faultless, idealizing him or her.	You add the new relationship to former ones. You are more realistic, admitting other's faults, but loving anyway.

8. How do others view you two? What's the attitude of friends and parents?	Few or none approve of the relationship.	Most or all approve. You get along well with other's friends and parents.
Dealing with double trouble		
9. What does distance (long separation) do to the relationship?	Withers away, dies; can't stand this added stress.	Survives; may even grow.
10. How do quarrels affect the romance?	They get more frequent, more severe, and will kill relationship.	They grow less frequent, less severe.
The inner world of love		
11. How do you feel about and refer to your relationship?	Much use of I/me/my; he/him/his; she/her/hers; little feeling of oneness.	Speak of we/us/our; feel and think as a unit, a pair; togetherness.
12. What's your ego response to the other?	Mainly selfish, restrictive; "What does this do for *me?*"	Mainly unselfish, releasing; concerned equally for other.
13. What's your overall attitude toward the other?	Attitude of taking; exploit and use the other.	Attitude of giving, sharing; want to serve other's needs, wants.
14. What is the effect of jealousy?	More frequent, more severe.	Less frequent, less severe.
TOTAL PATTERN OF THE CLUES	Kid stuff; puppy love.	The real thing; true love.

Summary clue: In real love you love the person so much that you want them to be happy—even if you may not be allowed to share their happiness.

that suggests a pretty solid love relationship. You can be encouraged. Your love is likely strong enough to support a successful marriage. The exceptions would be if you are still too young to marry, or if you have not yet passed the test of time—a minimum of two full years of knowing each other well. In any case, you will still want to "make haste slowly" and take whatever precautions you feel might be needed.

Scores between 50 and 90 points would indicate a toss-up between love and pseudo-love. Your relationship shows some promise. Take more time to see which direction it goes. It may in time grow into love.

If your score is less than 50, you are infatuated. Love is a very long way off. So take special care not to commit yourself very much to the relationship. Make no promises for the future. Be sure that reason rules emotion—and don't let yourself get heavily involved in sex. Love may grow in time. You can rate your romance later to see if you detect any change. But above all, don't rush into anything.

Meaning of scores

Score	Likely meaning	Action suggested
0-50	Infatuation	No promises; don't commit yourself
50-90	Toss-up	Some hope; give it more time
90-130	Real love	Ponder marriage— with due care

So now you know

Your score should give you a general idea of the nature of your romance. The next question is: What

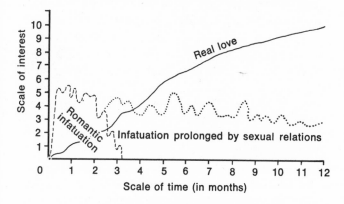

General life spans of infatuation and love compared

Scale of interest · Scale of time (in months)

Real love

Romantic infatuation

Infatuation prolonged by sexual relations

should you do about it? Based on what you've learned, what kind of future does your romance probably have? It may help if we contrast the expected life spans of infatuation and love on a graph.

The chart above does not reflect the fine details of a particular romance. Its purpose is to provide a general picture of typical romances.

As we have seen, infatuation starts fast. The level of interest in the romance comes and goes, with lots of peaks and valleys. If the couple steers clear of heavy sexual involvement, infatuation does not last long. It grinds to a rather abrupt halt, unless real love emerges in the meantime.

If the couple allows a sex life to develop and both find it satisfying, interest in sex may keep the romance going for many months—even up to four or five years. But it will end eventually. Meanwhile, the couple's interest will continue to blow hot and cold. The grave danger is that the couple involved in sex likely won't

161

be able to tell whether it's real love or just interest in sex that is holding them together—unless they arrange to be apart for a few months to test it out.

Love starts more slowly and grows as time goes by. The rough spots in the couple's early relationship slowly even out. Their interest keeps growing to a high level that they can maintain for years—even a lifetime. They come to count on their relationship being stable, secure, and satisfying.

The romance risk

It should now be quite clear why "romantic love"—infatuation—is such a dangerous myth. If you marry on the strength of it, you take a terrible risk. Even if you add sex thrills to the infatuation equation, there is bound to be trouble ahead. Sex just prolongs the agony a little longer.

Granted, some couples may luck out. By chance their personalities may in the long run grow to be compatible. They may have the basic elements that can later build into real love.

But why gamble? What if it turns out that they do not have the potential for love between them? Their marriage may well be doomed at the outset. Based as it is on romance alone, it will likely falter, fade, and finally fail.

Romantic infatuation, the state most people call "love," is pseudo-love, a cheap substitute for the real thing. It lures its innocent victims to the altar, then dashes their lovely hopes in the marital mud.

Does all this mean you should shun all romantic infatuations? Are they all bad? Must you deny yourself all those nice, warm, romantic feelings and pleasures? Not at all.

Infatuations are fine, *but*—

A good, lively infatuation can be a grand and glorious thing. It can lift you to the clouds and open whole new horizons. It can help you tap deep feelings and tender emotions that you never dreamed you could have. This is an emotional trip that each of us should take at least once in life.

So when it hits you, don't fight it. Relax. Let it sweep over you like a warm wave at the bathing beach. Just be sure you don't let that wave of emotion drown your good sense. And most important of all, *don't do anything drastic about it right away.* Don't do anything foolish. By that we mean two things.

First, be sure you don't get swept into some "quickie commitment" that you might later regret. By all means, take lots of time. Remind yourself that if the real stuff of love is to be found in your relationship, it will still be there next week and next month—and next year. No need to hurry into anything. You can never go wrong by taking your time. If your love is real, it will not fade. You can afford to be cautious, to wait. Be slow even to label it love. Above all, remind yourself that infatuation is never enough to build a marriage on.

Second, don't be too quick to get involved in sex. You will no doubt want very much to have sex. That is quite normal. The urge may at times seem too strong to curb. But sex can lead to a whole flock of new and needless complications. It can dull your ability to think straight about your relationship.

So wait for sex until after you have a firm grip on your feelings. Wait until you are quite sure that you really care about each other in a very dear way before you let much sex get into the act.

Infatuation may grow into love

If you determine that you're infatuated, not in love, you don't have to rush to end the relationship. Infatuation can and sometimes does develop into real love. If you sever a relationship the instant your realize it is—at that point—only infatuation, how will you ever know whether it would have grown into real love? Assume a wait-and-see attitude. If it doesn't last, fine. You have made no rash commitments, and you haven't dashed into sex, so you need have no regrets. If and when the break does come, you can much more easily accept it.

Breaking it up

After you've given a relationship a fair trial and you're convinced that it's an infatuation with no future, you may want to call it quits. If you decide to do that, of course, try not to hurt your partner any more than you have to. In some cases Cupid's wounds cut pretty deep. Remove the arrow with great care. Be as nice about it as you can.

At the same time, you do the person no favor by putting off the breakup. That is cruel. As soon as you are sure of your decision, tell him or her right away. It may not come as much of a surprise. You have probably dropped some hints along the way that you had your doubts about the relationship.

In any case, *be perfectly honest—and gently firm.* If you see no future at all in the situation, make that quite clear. If there is no hope, offer the person none. And explain in full your reasons for the break. Remain friends if you care to. But be firm in your decision before you act, then stick by it if you feel you are right. Remember, if it's infatuation for both of you, you will both tend to get over it fairly fast.

If the person threatens you in anger, stall until you can get protective support from parents or friends. If he or she tries to hold on to you by threatening self-harm or even suicide, that is a bluff—unless the person is mentally sick. Even so, you cannot be held responsible for the immature reactions of others if you've done your best to be kind and considerate, yet truthful. A relationship that is continued under the pressure of threat is no relationship at all.

It's time to stop snickering

All of this is fine for the person who has found real love, or who is infatuated and knows it. But what if you have a friend who is in the throes of an infatuation and thinks it's love? Should you just ignore it and hope the person comes to his or her senses? Should you just not talk about it for fear of losing your good relationship with that person? That is the strong temptation, but is it right?

Some people just laugh it off. We have a curious quirk in our culture. We are amused when others are in discomfort or danger. We giggle at the guy who whacks his thumb with a hammer or the girl who has ripped an embarrassing hole in her swimsuit. We guffaw at the pitiful drunk when his coordination has been impaired by booze. We snicker at the youngster —or oldster—who is so smitten with romantic infatuation that he or she behaves like a fool.

Why should we laugh at the antics of one who has crippled his body and mind with alcohol? And why are we amused when persons become infatuated, lose their appetite, and flunk algebra? Or worse still, when they move quickly into marriage, even though the two of them have little or nothing in common?

Instead of laughing at an infatuated friend, maybe you ought to cry, or at least cry out—in solemn warning. What if you saw that same friend skiing toward a tree? If you knew—as we know with marriage—that the chances of tragedy were 50-50, would you laugh? Would we say without concern: "Well, it's Peg's life— if she wrecks it that's her business"?

Getting into a miserable marriage is far from funny. Maybe our first step toward a remedy is to stop laughing. Why not start talking sense to the persons involved?

Full freedom—to fail?

We live in one of the few places on this whole planet where youths are allowed full freedom to choose their own mates. In most cultures marriage is considered far too important to be left to the inexperienced young. The choice of partners is made by families or matchmakers. The decision is based on reason, not romance. If love develops at all, it comes after the marriage, not before. Most cultures see "romantic love" as a condition that is "here today but gone tomorrow." Hence it is thought to be far too frail a foundation for marriage. Such a system may seem strange to us, but these cultures have very few marriages that fail.

In the best arranged marriages, care is taken that the couple will be compatible, that they are a good match. This assures that the couple will have lots of things in common. It gives them a firm base for getting along well. Of course, it has an obvious defect. It robs the couple of their own free choice. They have to take what they get.

On the other hand, marriages based on romance, such as those in America, allow people full freedom to choose their own mates. Once they are of age, they are free to act on their own best judgment. They can—and often do—ignore the wishes of families, friends, and everyone else.

Yet a couple may pay a high price for that freedom. "Romantic love" (infatuation) doesn't last long. It's flimsy and fickle. Then, too, the couple's eyes are often so full of stars that they fail to see the true nature of each other. Their pink cloud is often shrouded in fog. They may skip over many important facts that ought to be considered in their decision. The chances for their mating success are therefore much reduced.

Now, I do not suggest a return to the arranged marriage. That would never catch on in our freedom-loving Western world. But I do think there's a better way to choose mates. We can preserve the best values from both systems of mate choice, and at the same time avoid their risks.

How to have your wedding cake and eat it too

How can you have the best of both worlds? For one thing, you can be careful to match up the main factors in your own personality and background with those of a likely mate. Give it careful thought. Then you can seriously consult your family and friends about the person you think might be a good choice—and listen with great care to what they say. You can make use of test scores and computer results. You can master the 14 clues and become expert in the art of using them. You can see what social science has already

167

found out about how to tell real love from romantic fool's gold.

If you do these things well, you can have your wedding cake and eat it too. You can preserve your right to choose, yet glean most of the benefits of the more stable arranged marriage. In brief, you can apply realism and good sense to your problem.

Two + *tu* + true = one

This may sound like terrible math, but it's actually a good formula for sound mate choice.

The French have two words that mean "you"—*vous* and *tu*. They use *vous* when they speak to someone they don't know very well. They use *tu* if the person is a beloved friend or relative.

So here's the proper mix for a good marriage. Take *two* normal, mature persons. Add a close *tu* relationship (with or without romantic infatuation). Then stir in generous helpings of their own good sense, and chill with the *true* findings of science. Mix the ingredients well. This will produce a happy, lasting union with strong bonds.

If followed with due care, this formula could bring a dramatic change in the rates of marital failure in every society where romance is now the main basis for mating. This is a recipe you can bet your life on. And when it comes right down to it, that's exactly what you're doing when you wed—you're betting your life.

The sacred right to co-create

One of the great privileges of marriage is to have children. It is a sacred right. Did you ever take a close look at a newborn baby? So tiny, so fragile, so precious, so full of promise for the future. Tagore, the Indian poet, once said that every time a baby is born it is a sign that God has not yet lost hope for his world. It is indeed a miracle of miracles.

And just think—you and the one you come to love can claim the right to help create another human being. What a sacred trust! What a joy when that tiny babe comes as a gift from God, with the full blessing of society and loved ones.

But how sobering to think that those two little eyes never would have opened if you two had not known intimacy. Those tiny fingers and hands would never have touched if you had not shared with each other. That little mind would never have thought and reasoned and willed without the love of you and your mate.

What a responsibility! No wonder my old teacher, Hornell Hart, used to furrow his brow at us and exclaim: "How dare you look upon sex as just a plaything!"

How dare we, indeed. In a time when we are rediscovering and stressing the joys and pleasures of sex, there is grave danger that we will fail to grasp the deeper meaning of sex—the sacred right to co-create. Sex is a joy, but it's not a toy. It is not a privilege to be taken lightly. It should be an act of loving, of caring and sharing. In its fullest meaning, sex is a sacred ritual through which two human personalities are joined in every part of their being. I hope you find that kind of sharing.

Have a rich love—and a happy life.

Notes

Chapter 1

1. William M. Kephart, *The Family, Society and the Individual,* 3rd ed. (Boston: Houghton Mifflin, 1972), p. 349.

2. Paul Popenoe, "The Romantic Complex," *Family Life Magazine.*

3. *Good News for Modern Man: The New Testament in Today's English Version,* 2nd ed. (New York: American Bible Society, 1966), 1 Corinthians 13:4-7.

4. William Proxmire, Senator from Wisconsin, press release dated March 11, 1975. See also reply by Ellen Berscheid, professor of psychology, University of Minnesota at Minneapolis, in John W. Kole, "Proxmire Barb Goes Unloved," *Milwaukee Journal,* 11 March 1975, p. 4. She "said that Senator Proxmire was trying to turn back the clock by criticizing valid research about love. 'Sen. Proxmire himself has suffered marital separation. I would think that he especially would want to understand about love being the basis for the marriage contract.' Proxmire, 59, announced last month that he and his wife, Ellen, had reached a reconciliation after more than 3½ years of separation."

5. Merton P. Strommen, *Five Cries of Youth* (New York: Harper and Row, 1974), p. 25.

6. Dianne Kieren, June Henton, and Rainona Marotz, *His and Hers: A Problem Solving Approach to Marriage* (Hinsdale, Ill.: The Dryden Press, 1975), p. 50.

7. Albert Ellis, "Love and Family Relationships of American College Girls," *The American Journal of Sociology* 55 (May 1950): 554.

8. Kephart, *Family*, p. 347. For findings relative to that study, see William M. Kephart, "Some Correlates of Romantic Love," *Journal of Marriage and the Family* 29 (August 1967): 470-474; and "The 'Dysfunctional' Theory of Romantic Love: A Research Report," *Journal of Comparative Family Studies* 1 (Autumn 1970): 26-36.

9. Ernest W. Burgess, Paul Wallin, and Gladys Denny Shultz, *Courtship, Engagement and Marriage* (Philadelphia: Lippincott, 1954), p. 136.

10. Gilbert V. Hamilton, *A Research in Marriage* (New York: Albert and Charles Boni, 1929); Clifford Kirkpatrick and Theodor Caplow, "Emotional Trends in the Courtship Experience of College Students as Expressed by Graphs with Some Observations on Methodological Implications," *American Sociological Review* 10:5 (October 1945): 619.

11. Leonard Benson, *The Family Bond: Marriage, Love and Sex in America* (New York: Random House, 1971), p. 116.

12. Kephart, *Family*, p. 348.

13. Benson, *Family Bond*, p. 116.

14. D. G. Dean, "Romanticism and Emotional Maturity: A Further Exploration," *Social Forces* 42 (March 1964): 298-303. See William L. Kolb, "Family Sociology, Marriage Education, and the Romantic Complex," *Social Forces* 29 (October 1950): 65-72.

15. Andreas Capellanus, *The Art of Courtly Love*, abr. and ed., Frederick W. Locke (New York: Frederick Ungar Publishing Co., 1957), p. 4; also in William N. Stephens, ed., *Reflections on Marriage* (New York: Thomas Y. Crowell, 1968), p. 42.

Chapter 2

1. Henry A. Bowman, *Marriage for Moderns*, 7th ed. (New York: McGraw-Hill, 1974), p. 107.

2. Raoul de Roussy de Sales, "Love in America," *Atlantic Monthly* 161 (May 1938): 645.

3. Ross Stagner, *Psychology of Personality*, 2nd ed. (New York: McGraw-Hill, 1948), p. 379.

4. Robert Wernick and the editors of Time-Life Books, *The Family* (New York: Time-Life Books, 1974), p. 8.

5. Paul Popenoe and Donna Wicks, "Marital Happiness in Two Generations," *Mental Hygiene* 21 (April 1937) 218-33.

See also Lewis M. Terman, *et al., Psychological Factors in Marital Happiness* (New York: McGraw-Hill, 1938); Ernest W. Burgess and Leonard S. Cottrell, *Predicting Success or Failure in Marriage* (Englewood Cliffs, N.J.: Prentice-Hall, 1939), p. 34; Eustace Chesser, *et al., The Sexual, Marital, and Family Relationships with English Women* (New York: Roy, 1957); and Judson T. and Mary G. Landis, *Building a Successful Marriage*, 6th ed. (Englewood Cliffs, N.J.: Prentice-Hall, 1973), pp. 6, 9.

6. Lloyd Saxton, *The Individual, Marriage, and the Family*, 2nd ed. (Belmont, Calif.: Wadsworth Publishing Co., 1972), p. 165. See also Paul C. Glick, *American Families* (New York: John Wiley and Sons, 1957); Hugh Carter and Paul C. Glick, *Marriage and Divorce: A Social and Economic Study* (Cambridge, Mass.: Harvard University Press, 1970), pp. 38-39.

7. Alan E. Bayer, "Early Dating and Early Marriage," *Journal of Marriage and the Family* 30 (November 1968): 631.

8. William F. Pratt, *A Study of Marriages Involving Premarital Pregnancies,* Dissertation, Department of Sociology, University of Michigan, 1965.

9. Horace Gary, "Courtship and Conception," *Medical Times* 89 (July 1961): 677-80.

10. Saxton, *Individual and Family,* p. 166.

11. Robert F. Winch, *The Modern Family,* rev. ed. (New York: Henry Holt, 1964). Also Saxton, *Individual and Family,* p. 166.

12. "Too Young," words by Sylvia Dee, music by Sid Lippman, Jefferson Music Co., 1951.

13. David H. Knox Jr. and Michael J. Sporakowski, "Attitudes of College Students Toward Love," *Journal of Marriage and the Family* 30 (November 1968): 638-42. See also Benson, *Family Bond,* p. 116, and Kephart, "Some Correlates," pp. 569-78.

14. Burgess and Cottrell, *Predicting Success,* 1939. See also Landis and Landis, *Building a Successful Marriage,* pp. 6, 90-94; and Judson T. Landis, "The Pattern of Divorce in Three Generations," *Social Forces* 34:3 (March 1956): 213-16; and Juliette L. Despert, *Children of Divorce,* 1st ed. (Garden City, New York: Doubleday, 1962), preface.

15. Saxton, *Individual and Family,* p. 165.

16. Nancy Moore Clatworthy, "Living Together," in Nona Glazer-Malbin, *Old Family/New Family: Interpersonal Relationships* (New York: D. Van Nostrand Co., 1975), pp. 67-89.

17. Judith Lyness, Milton Lipetz, and Keith Davis, "Living

Together: An Alternative to Marriage," *Journal of Marriage and the Family* 34 (May 1972): 305-12.

18. Eleanor D. Macklin, "Heterosexual Cohabitation among Unmarried College Students," *Family Coordinator* (October 1972): 463-471.

Chapter 3

1. Denis de Rougemont, *Love in the Western World* (New York: Harcourt, Brace & Co., 1940), pp. 75-76.

2. Wendell Johnson, *People in Quandaries* (New York: Harper and Brothers, 1946), pp. 14-20.

3. William Graham Cole, *Sex and Love in the Bible* (New York: Association Press, 1959), p. 53.

4. C. S. Lewis, *The Four Loves* (London: Geoffrey Bles, 1960), p. 106.

5. Theodor Reik, *Of Love and Lust: On the Psychoanalysis of Romantic and Sexual Emotions* (New York: Farrar, Straus and Cudahy, 1957), especially Part 1.

6. Unpublished work by P. K. Houdek provides much of the basic framework for these 14 clues.

Chapter 4

1. Robert R. and P. L. Bell, "Sexual Satisfaction Among Married Women," *Medical Aspects of Human Sexuality* 6 (December 1972): 136-144. Also Alfred C. Kinsey and others, *Sexual Behavior in the Human Male* (Philadelphia: Saunders, 1948); and *Sexual Behavior in the Human Female,* 1953.

Chapter 5

1. Landis and Landis, *Building Marriage,* p. 166-67.

2. Zick Rubin, *Liking and Loving: An Invitation to Social Psychology* (New York: Holt, Rinehart and Winston, 1973), p. 113.

Chapter 7

1. James Leslie McCary, *Freedom and Growth in Marriage* (Santa Barbara, Calif.: Hamilton Publishing Co., 1975), p. 137.

Chapter 8

1. Shirley Lord, "Conversation About Being in Love," *Harper's Bazaar* 103 (May 1970): 60.
2. Robert K. Kelly, *Courtship, Marriage, and the Family* (New York: Harcourt, Brace and World, Inc., 1969), p. 213.
3. Reik, *Of Love*, p. 80.
4. J. L. and Alma L. Hirning, *Marriage Adjustment* (New York: American Book Co., 1956), p. 123; Evelyn M. Duvall and Reuben Hill, *When You Marry*, rev. ed. (New York: Association Press, 1953), pp. 40-41, 43.
5. *Ibid.*, p. 30.
6. Landis and Landis, *Building Marriage*, pp. 119-20.

Chapter 10

1. Bowman, *Marriage for Moderns*, pp. 39-43.
2. Paul Gebhard, "Accent on the News," *Milwaukee Journal*, February 20, 1977, p. 1.
3. Harold T. Christensen and Christina F. Gregg, "Changing Sex Norms in America and Scandinavia," *Journal of Marriage and Family* 32 (November 1970): 616-27. See also Robert R. Bell and Michael Gordon, *The Social Dimensions of Human Sexuality* (Boston: Little, Brown and Co., 1972), pp. 51-59.
4. Richard F. Hettlinger, *Living with Sex: The Student's Dilemma* (New York: Seabury Press, 1966), chapter 10.
5. Bell and Gordon, *Social Dimensions*, pp. 51-53. See also Kinsey and others, *Sexual Behavior in the Human Male*, p. 364.
6. Ernest Burgess and Paul Wallin, *Engagement and Marriage* (Philadelphia: J. B. Lippincott Co., 1953).
7. *Ibid.*
8. Kinsey and others, *Sexual Behavior in the Human Female*, pp. 427-28.
9. Shere Hite, *The Hite Report: A Nationwide Study of Female Sexuality* (New York: Dell Publishing Co., Inc., 1976), p. 229: "Only approximately 30% of the women in this study could orgasm regularly from intercourse."
10. Radio interview, WBBM Chicago, October 25, 1977.
11. Elaine C. Pierson, *Sex Is Never an Emergency: A Candid Guide for Young Adults*, 3rd ed. (Philadelphia: J. B. Lippincott Co., 1973).

Chapter 11

1. See also Bryan Green, "A Basis for Sex Morality," Part 6, a filmstrip (Malibu, Calif.: Stephen Bosustow Productions).

2. H.W. Long, *Sane Sex Life and Sane Sex Living* (New York: Oak Press, 1961).

Chapter 13

1. Elsie King, "Personality Characteristics . . . Ideal and Perceived in Relation to Mate Selection," unpublished Ph.D. dissertation, Libraries of the University of Southern California, 1961.

2. Walter Stephan, Ellen Berscheid, and Elaine Walster, "Sexual Arousal and Heterosexual Perception," *Journal of Personality and Social Psychology* 20 (October 1971): 93-101.

3. Sidney M. Jourard and Ardis Whitman, "The Fear That Cheats Us of Love," *Redbook* 137 (October 1971): 82-83.

4. Robert O. Blood Jr., *Marriage*, 2nd ed. (New York: The Free Press, 1969), p. 112.

Chapter 14

1. Landis and Landis, *Building Marriage*, p. 117.

2. Kelly, *Courtship*, p. 217.

3. Richard Driscoll, Keith E. Davis, and Milton E. Lipetz, "Parental Interference and Romantic Love: The Romeo and Juliet Effect," *Journal of Personality and Social Psychology* 24 (October 1972): 1-10.

4. Harvey J. Locke, *Predicting Adjustment in Marriage: A Comparison of a Divorced and a Happily Married Group* (New York: Henry Holt and Co., Inc., 1951), pp. 75-76.

Chapter 16

1. George R. Bach and Ronald M. Deutsch, "Conflict: The Key to Sustained Reality" in Carl E. Williams and John F. Crosby, *Choice and Challenge: Contemporary Readings in Marriage* (Dubuque, Iowa: William C. Brown Co., 1974), p. 182.

2. Murray A. Strauss, "Leveling, Civility, and Violence in the Family," *Journal of Marriage and Family* 36 (February 1974).

Chapter 17

1. Reik, *Of Love*, p. 73.

2. Hirning and Hirning, *Marriage Adjustment*, p. 121; Reik, *Of Love*, p. 71.

Chapter 18

1. Reik, *Of Love,* p. 20.
2. Hirning and Hirning, *Marriage Adjustment,* p. 282.
3. Luke 17:33, *Today's English Version.*
4. The Registry for Planetary Citizenship is at: Planetary Citizens, 777 United Nations Plaza, New York, N.Y. 10017.

Chapter 19

1. Reik, *Of Love,* pp. 101-102.
2. Blood, *Marriage,* p. 108.

Chapter 20

1. George P. Murdock, *Social Structure* (New York: Free Press, 1965), p. 294. Also William N. Stephens, *Comparative Perspectives on Marriage and the Family* (New York: Holt, Rinehart and Winston, 1963), p. 59; and Arlene S. Skolnick, *The Intimate Environment: Exploring Marriage and the Family* (Boston: Little, Brown, 1973), pp. 256-59.
2. Skolnick, *Intimate Environment,* pp. 253-56.
3. McCary, *Freedom and Growth,* p. 48.
4. Philip Nobile, "Uncommon Conversations: A Vote for the 'New Fidelity,'" from *Insight Magazine,* in the *Milwaukee Journal,* 13 November 1977, pp. 28, 31.
5. Margaret Mead in Aron M. Krich, ed., *The Anatomy of Love* (New York: Dell Publishing Co., 1960).
6. Skolnick, *Intimate Environment,* p. 259.
7. Locke, *Predicting Adjustment,* p. 153.
8. Blood, *Marriage,* p. 107.